LIKE THE SHEPHERD

LIKE THE SHEPHERD

LEADING YOUR MARRIAGE WITH LOVE AND GRACE

ROBERT WOLGEMUTH

FOREWORD BY NANCY DeMOSS WOLGEMUTH

REGNERY
FAITH

Regnery Faith™ is a trademark of Salem Communications Holding Corporation; Regnery® is a registered trademark of Salem Communications Holding Corporation

Scripture quotations are from the following sources:

The Holy Bible, English Standard Version® (ESV®)
Copyright © 2001 by Crossway,
A publishing ministry of Good News Publishers.
All rights reserved.

The Living Bible
Copyright © 1971. Used by permission of Tyndale House Publishers, Inc., Carol Stream, Illinois 60188. All rights reserved.

Cataloging-in-Publication data on file with the Library of Congress

ISBN 978-1-62157-511-5

Published in the United States by
Regnery Faith
An imprint of Regnery Publishing
A Division of Salem Media Group
300 New Jersey Ave NW
Washington, DC 20001
www.RegneryFaith.com

Manufactured in the United States of America

10 9 8 7 6 5 4 3 2 1

Books are available in quantity for promotional or premium use. For information on discounts and terms, please visit our website: www.Regnery.com.

Distributed to the trade by
Perseus Distribution
www.perseusdistribution.com

Published in association with the literary agency of Wolgemuth & Associates, Inc.

To Arthur S. DeMoss

With deepest appreciation, this book is dedicated to a man I never had the joy of meeting. His untimely death occurred in 1979 on the weekend of his oldest daughter's—my wife Nancy's—twenty-first birthday. Art's wife Nancy and their seven children have greatly missed his physical presence and his love and leadership. But Art DeMoss left an indelible imprint on each of them, and also on the lives of countless thousands around the world who came to faith in Christ through his personal witness. This man was a good shepherd to his wife, his family, and many others. I am deeply grateful for his example.

CONTENTS

FOREWORD

BY NANCY DeMoss WOLGEMUTH

To say that falling in love at the age of fifty-six was unexpected would be a huge understatement. Though I had been a strong champion of the institution of marriage and had never ruled out the possibility of marriage for myself, I had always had a strong sense of being set apart and called to serve the Lord as a single woman. Throughout my adult life, marriage simply had not been on my radar.

All that changed the day a certain gentleman expressed interest in pursuing a relationship with me. Much to my amazement and that of everyone who knew me, my heart was drawn to say yes. That man was Robert Wolgemuth, a widower whom I had known professionally as my literary agent a dozen years earlier.

Thus began a journey that led to our marriage nine months later. It all unfolded in a way that neither of us ever could have scripted. But God gave us peace throughout the process, as we trusted that He was writing this story and directing our steps.

The image of a shepherd was a prominent and recurring theme from the outset of our relationship. In our conversations and text messages, we often referred to the Lord as our Shepherd and invoked His wisdom, guidance, provision, and care. So much so, that "our song" soon became "Savior, Like a Shepherd Lead Us." It continues to be the prayer of our hearts that our Savior would lead us and that we would know His voice and gladly follow Him.

Early on, I learned that the biblical model of the Good Shepherd was the template for Robert's understanding of a husband's calling. In one of our very first phone conversations, reflecting on his forty-four-year marriage to his late wife, Bobbie, Robert said, almost in passing: "I loved being married, because I loved shepherding my wife."

Those words nearly took my breath away. I was struck that he didn't say he loved being married because of something his wife did for him, some need she met in his life. Rather, this man loved being married because he loved serving, blessing, caring and providing for, meeting the needs of, and gently leading his wife. He loved being a shepherd.

Seldom if ever have I heard another man describe himself or his marriage in that way. My heart was captured. Before long, this strong woman, the founder and leader of a national ministry who had spent years shepherding others, found herself willing and desiring to follow this man and to be shepherded by him.

Inexperienced as I was in matters of love and marriage, it helped that I had grown up in a home with a dad who had a shepherd's heart. Art DeMoss took seriously his responsibility to follow Christ and to lead his family to do the same. He prioritized the needs of his family above the relentless demands of his successful business. He lived out the exhortation found in the book of Proverbs: "Know well the condition of your flocks, and give attention to your herds" (27:23). So I knew what it was to trust an earthly shepherd.

As I contemplated marriage, which I knew would require an enormous adjustment, I felt I could trust Robert's heart because I saw him daily, earnestly, humbly seeking to follow our Shepherd. I knew Robert would not be a perfect husband (any more than I would be a perfect wife), but I knew I could trust our Shepherd to lead our home through this human shepherd.

Robert wrote this book during the first year of our marriage. Can you imagine the joy of being married to a man whose early morning hours were spent unpacking what it means for a husband to shepherd his wife? (I figured my part was to make sure he had plenty of real life illustrations!) He is a loving, caring, tender shepherd who has won my heart and has given me the joy of letting him lead, a man who seeks daily to follow the leadership of the Great Shepherd.

My prayer is that this book will help you better understand and live out your calling to reflect the heart of that same Great Shepherd in your marriage and family, to lay down your life for those He has entrusted to your care. I can assure you that, with rare exceptions, this is something your wife longs for and that she will likely respond to that kind of grace-filled, loving leadership in ways you may never have dreamed possible.

It is no secret that the majority of Christian books are purchased by women. If you are a husband, there's a good chance your wife put this book in your hands. (Or perhaps you're not even holding it—rather, you're listening to your wife read it to you!)

If you're a wife, I would say simply, "Let your husband shepherd you." Encourage and affirm him when he takes even small steps in that direction. And when he fails (as he will, and as you will), be patient, and extend to him the mercy, forgiveness, and grace that you want and need him to grant to you.

This is not to say you do not have a voice in your marriage or that you ought to mindlessly follow wherever your husband leads. Robert is eager to know my thoughts, perspective, and desires—on everything. He welcomes my input on issues big and small and is quick to thank me for it, even if it runs counter to what he was thinking. He is motivated to serve me, to honor me, and to lay down his life for me in the warp and woof of everyday life. I am a blessed woman.

He also knows that if after talking and seeking the Lord together on a matter, we have a different sense of the direction we should take, he has a wife who will support his leadership. This requires faith on both our parts. Faith in our Shepherd. At times, it requires me to be still and to wait on the Lord, trusting Him to move in Robert's heart. (I'm sure that goes for him as well.)

Many marriages are stuck in unhealthy or sinful patterns. In some cases, the dysfunction is acute and goes back for decades. This may describe your marriage. You may feel there is no chance you and your mate will ever enjoy the kind of healthy, loving, respectful relationship Robert writes about. You may be convinced the issues in your marriage will never be solved until your mate sees the light and changes.

I've often heard Robert stress how important it is for someone in the marriage to be willing to "go first" in obeying God. I don't know what script God is writing for your marriage; but I do believe that if you are willing to "go first" in applying the truths found in this book, in time you will find the dance step changing in your relationship and in your home. And even if your spouse never changes, if you trust your Good Shepherd and are determined to follow Him, you can be confident that He will care for you and meet your needs as only He can do.

I sat down to write this foreword late one night in the midst of a week that was jam-packed with other deadlines and projects. I ended up getting a second wind and working through the night. Needless to say, Robert was more than a little surprised when he came downstairs at 4:30 a.m. to start his day in the Word and prayer and I was still working away at my laptop. I sensed his concern about the toll that an all-nighter would take on my well-being. He knelt at my side and prayed as we do together at the start of each new day. He closed his prayer by saying tenderly, "And Lord, please help me to know how to protect and shepherd this woman." At which point, he urged me to head up to bed and get some sleep!

The heart expressed in that simple prayer meant more to me, even in my sleep-deprived state, than he could have realized. What a sweet sense of security, gratitude, and peace it brought to my heart. And what heightened desire to bless this precious man and to love him well.

A husband can hardly imagine what it means to his wife to hear him pray that kind of prayer on her behalf, for him to acknowledge that he can't do this on his own, that he needs direction and help (something I've been told some men find it difficult to ask for!), and that he is looking to the Shepherd of his soul to provide what he needs to shepherd the wife He has entrusted to his care.

Robert and I are praying for you as you read these pages and as you seek to lead your marriage with love and grace. May He give you a heart "like the Shepherd."

Nancy DeMoss Wolgemuth
March 2017

PREFACE

Here's an exciting way to start a book...a little English lesson. Ready? The word "shepherd" is both a noun and a verb. It's who you are and it's what you do.

In your marriage, you are the shepherd—a noun. And the way you succeed at the task is to shepherd—a verb. Class dismissed.

If you had lived in Chicago's western suburbs in the late fifties or sixties or seventies and were looking for a Pontiac, the chances are you would have bought your car from Eddie Ruch (pronounced "roosh"), a premier dealership for the Pontiac brand in the Midwest and a respected anchor in the Wheaton business community.

Visiting this establishment was a treat for me as a car-loving teenager. Even before I earned my driver's license in 1964, I had visited the Eddie Ruch showroom on Front Street in downtown Wheaton with my dad many times. Gleaming vehicles sitting quietly on a polished showroom floor, the smell of new cars…what could be more awe-inspiring for a boy?

In 1958 Dad bought the family a brand new green four-door Catalina from Eddie Ruch. The Catalina was the less expensive model with fewer bells and whistles. He would have liked a Bonneville but felt that a man in ministry should opt for less pretension. By 1964, however, Dad seemed to have worked through his apprehension about showing off, and he bought the Bonneville just in time for my senior year in high school. Because the car was for a family of eight, it was another four-door. Not as sleek as the two-door, but terrific anyway.

Driving the streets of my hometown by myself gave me a euphoric sense of independence, a taste of being a man. The windows were rolled down, which meant that I could hang my left arm out and lay it against the door. This was "the look." It was cool. And I was cool.

Meeting Eddie Ruch

In the summer of 1961, I was playing touch football with my buddies in our backyard. The air was dense. Weighty. But for boys, this didn't matter. Just a few hundred feet away was the intersection of Roosevelt Road and Main Street. Suddenly our game was interrupted by the sound of horns blowing and tires screeching. And then the sounds came to an abrupt stop with a heavy thud, followed immediately by the sound of shattering glass. A car had run the stop sign on Main Street. As boys would do, we raced to get a closer look.

Fortunately, no one was seriously injured. Since this intersection was only a few blocks from Front Street, a wrecker from Eddie Ruch Pontiac was called to the scene. The truck arrived, backing up to one of the cars, sitting crossways in the middle of the intersection. Steam was hissing from the car's radiator, sending a thin plume of whiteness into the air.

I watched as a short, bald man with thick glasses, large ears, and a huge smile stepped out of the truck's cab and went quickly to work. The sleeves of his sweat-stained shirt were rolled up above his elbows, and we guessed that this wasn't his first call of the day. The street was blocked by the cars, so he wasted no time, pulling the large chain from the truck bed and climbing under the car with the chain's hooked end.

Soon the man emerged from under the car and returned to the tow truck. He pulled one of the levers, starting a winch. The chain tightened, carefully lifting the front tires of the damaged car off the road. I loved this part. The diminutive man pushing the levers was quietly in charge.

And then, for the first time, I noticed a patch on his shirt pocket with the words "Eddie Ruch Pontiac" and another with his first name.

"Eddie."

Just Eddie.

You're ahead of me on this, aren't you? That's right. The man with the sweet smile, the firm calloused hands, and the black grease tucked around the edges of each of his fingernails was Eddie Ruch himself. The tow truck, the shiny new cars, the service department, and the whole dealership belonged to him.

If your car broke down and you needed a tow, Eddie Ruch was your guy. But if you went into his showroom to buy a new Pontiac, Eddie was nowhere to be seen. Instead, you would have been helped by Art Vanasek, friendly and square-jawed handsome, his thick dark hair combed straight back, his shirt white and perfectly laundered. He had a way with customers, including my dad. For many years Art was one of Pontiac's premier salesmen.

Both Eddie and Art seemed happy with this unconventional division of labor, and from all appearances it worked well.

The Head of Your Home

Many people don't read a book's preface, but clearly you're the exception. The story about Eddie Ruch and Art Vanasek is foundational to understanding what I'm going to say in the pages that follow. The memory of these two came to mind after a conversation with my wife, Nancy, about the title and subtitle of this book. We were talking about the word "leading."

Of course she knew I was writing a book with the phrase "leading your marriage" on the cover.

It reminded me of the Apostle Paul's one-sentence summary of the way everything is supposed to be in our marriage: "But I want you to understand that the head of every man is Christ, the head of a wife is her husband, and the head of Christ is God." (1 Corinthians 11:3) So is there a difference between *heading* and *leading*, I wondered. Sometimes they're the same. Sometimes they're not.

> A PONTIAC DEALERSHIP NEEDS AN OWNER. A SHEPHERD. A HEAD. THE GUY WITH HIS NAME ON THE SIGN. SO DOES YOUR MARRIAGE.

That night, the story of Eddie Ruch woke me up. I couldn't wait to tell Nancy the next morning.

Art Vanasek was the leader of the Pontiac dealership, well suited—literally—to manage the company's sales, and he seemed to love what he did. Eddie was the head of the dealership. His primary responsibility was to empower Art to be successful. Eddie understood his own strengths and happily opted to drive the wrecker instead of wearing crisp white shirts and shiny dress shoes.

A Pontiac dealership needs an owner. A shepherd. A head. The guy with his name on the sign. So does your marriage.

You may not see yourself as a man with leadership skills, but you are still the head of your marriage and your home. That's the message of this book. And I'm letting you know right up front, in the preface. Now that you know where we're going, you may decide that such a message is not for you. Or for your marriage. If so, I understand. I really do.

But if the idea fascinates you, or if you believe that when the Bible speaks about something it's worth serious consideration—even embracing—then welcome to the experience.

My hope—my prayer—is that this book will help you on your way to a goal that you and I grasp in unison: that you'd grow to be more like Christ and that your marriage will be strengthened.

If this happens, the time you've spent reading will have been a worthwhile investment, and my mission will have been accomplished. How good would that be? Very good.

God bless you.

Robert Wolgemuth

INTRODUCTION

It's hard to believe you're reading a book about being a *shepherd*. Frankly, from a distance, this looks like a totally sissy thing.

You're a shepherd? I'm a shepherd?

Seriously?

At one point, I thought we should put a photo of a Harley or a rugby scrum on the cover. This would be especially helpful if you're reading this book on an airplane or over lunch in your company's break room. I mean, who wants the guy in the window seat or next to you at the table to look over and see a man—*a man*—reading a book about shepherds and sheep?

But because I believe in truth in advertising, I decided that the word "shepherd" needed to appear on the cover. This was the right thing to do.

It's in the Bible

Since 2009, I have begun every morning with the *One Year Bible*. As you may know, this edition of the Scriptures is organized with an Old Testament and a New Testament reading for each day. It also includes something from the Psalms and the Proverbs. My wife and children do the same, so we often text each other early in the day about what we've (virtually) read together.

The morning that I had scheduled to write the Introduction to this book, my daily reading included the twenty-third Psalm, which as you know begins, "The Lord is my Shepherd, I shall not want." Wow, I thought, this is amazing. Talk about a message from the Lord!

The New Testament reading included Jesus' words from Matthew 19:5 (quoting Genesis 2) about divorce: "Therefore a man shall leave his father and mother and hold fast to his wife, and the two shall be one flesh."

"Okay, I'm getting the message, Lord," I whispered.

But the kicker was the Old Testament reading, taken from Exodus 6 and 7. I read the story of God's call to Moses to go, at great risk to his own life, to Pharaoh, absolute potentate of Egypt, and demand that the Israelites be released from their captivity. This is one of the Bible's most graphic depictions of a man standing in the gap on behalf of someone else—in this case about a million someone elses, the Hebrew people.

I had read this account many times, but I had never appreciated the power of chapter 7, verse 1: "And the LORD said to Moses, 'See I have made you like God to Pharaoh, and your brother Aaron shall be your prophet. You shall speak all that I command you....'"

In those pre-dawn hours, the Lord now had my full attention. I was thinking, the Lord is my Shepherd ... my wife and I are one flesh.

"Before God and these witnesses," I have the responsibility and the privilege to be a strong advocate on behalf of my wife. In fact, with His call and His blessing, I can have a heart ... be a shepherd ... "like God" ... in my own home.

There was one more thing. You might remember that when God spoke to Moses in the bush that burned but was not consumed, He allowed the stammering, fearful Moses to take his brother along to plead his case to the Pharaoh. And God promised to go with Moses, giving Pharaoh little choice but to let the Hebrews go. When the Psalmist retells this story, he sings: "[God] struck down every firstborn in Egypt, the first-fruits of their strength in the tents of Ham. Then he led out his people like sheep and guided them in the wilderness like a flock. He led them in safety, so that they were not afraid, but the sea overwhelmed their enemies." (Psalm 78:51–53)

In the pages that follow, in the quest to understand what it means to have our very own Good Shepherd and to be a good shepherd to our wives, it would be a privilege to be your ally. Your brother. To go along with you like Aaron, to help and encourage you.

A Shepherd ... Are You Kidding Me?

Back to the crazy idea of being a shepherd to your wife ... I have a warning for you: even among Christians, the notion of shepherding—leading—your marriage may not go over well. Remember these verses from Ephesians?

> Wives, submit to your own husbands, as to the Lord. For the husband is the head of the wife even as Christ is the head of the church, his body, and is himself its Savior. Now

as the church submits to Christ, so also wives should submit in everything to their husbands. (5:22–24)

WHAT EXACTLY DOES "SUBMIT" MEAN IN THE TWENTY-FIRST CENTURY? AND HOW ABOUT THIS ONE: "THE HUSBAND IS THE HEAD OF THE WIFE." ARE YOU KIDDING ME?

In our contemporary world—even among Christians—there may be no passage that has been critically dissected more thoroughly than this one. What exactly does "submit" mean in the twenty-first century? And how about this one: "the husband is the head of the wife." Are you kidding me?

Publicly quoting these lines from Paul in a book is no way to win a popularity contest. I've even been accosted by folks (including a pastor in the church parking lot) after I taught these passages in Sunday school. So I'm ready, hunkered down in an undisclosed location.

Truth Be Told

I could go to the Internet to collect all kinds of statistics on the current state of marriage, but I'm not going to. I could gather data that confirms without question that the institution of marriage is broken. But I'm not going to do that either. Why? Because you and I already know it. Marriage is in peril.

Instead, let's pretend that I'm a football coach and you're the quarterback of my team. It's halftime of a big game. Our whole team has just trudged into the locker room, reeking of sweat and analgesic balm. But before the whole team gathers together for a pep talk, you and I are meeting in my office.

Oh, I didn't mention that the first half of this game has been a huge challenge. The local sport's writers had picked us to win this contest handily, but from the first snap until now, we have had our hands full. We've had some good moments but there have been some mistakes and setbacks.

But before I address all your discouraged teammates, we are meeting behind a closed door. It's just you and me. We do not sit down. We're both too nervous to sit down.

I look into your face. You know that I have a great deal of affection for you. You know that I believe in the quality of your skills, and above all, you know that I know that you want to do your best out there. But even without saying it, you and I also know the truth. And we agree.

What we're doing isn't working. And if we have a July snowflake's chance in the second half, we're going to have to deliver some serious encouragement to your teammates and yes, make some adjustments to our game plan.

The scoreboard is not lying. Marriage is hard work. The story of our struggles in the first half has already been submitted to the sports pages. Bloggers are blogging. Twitterers are tweeting. Everyone knows about our spotty performance and some pundits are skeptical that we're going to able to pull this one off. The message is clear. We can use some help.

And so, in these precious moments before walking into the locker room to give our team some hope and encouragement, I lay the game plan—the Bible—on my desk. Gently tapping its cover, I tell you, "This is how this game was supposed to be played. I've seen many teams use it before. When they've followed this plan, they have won." I look straight into your face and you look into mine. You know that I'm in this thing with you. You hear my words and you know that I'm serious about the power and veracity of this strategy.

As we finish our conversation, I give you a reassuring side-winder hug and a swat on your backside. You and I both know that we have to go back to the plan. And we're going to have to follow it as though the outcome depends on it.

Because it does.

So, even though you and I know that the approach I'm taking in this book...the presupposition I'm making in quoting these verses... is going to be met with stout opposition, we know something else for sure.

This Shepherd and Sheep Thing

By the time you read this Introduction, I will have been married for almost forty-six years. My story may be a little different from yours, because I have not been married to just one woman. Bobbie, my wife of forty-four and a half years, stepped into heaven in 2014 after a thirty-month battle with cancer. In His kindness, the Lord graced me with a second wife, named Nancy.

BOBBIE AND NANCY BOTH BELIEVED THAT THEIR HUSBAND WAS CALLED BY GOD TO BE THEIR LEADER, THEIR HEAD, THEIR EARTHLY SHEPHERD. I HAD NO CHOICE ABOUT THE THEME OF THIS BOOK.

Bobbie and Nancy were friends. These two women, both incredibly capable and smart, had three fundamental things in common: they both loved Jesus with all their hearts, they both loved me as their husband and told me so all the time, and they both believed the Bible's teaching on marriage and the message of this book: "Let your husband lead." It's an irony that defies explanation, but each of these gifted women has spoken, believed, taught, and even written these words in books.

They did this because they both believed that it was the only halftime challenge that had any chance at all to work. In fact, they both were so committed to this approach to marriage that they repeated these words countless times to women who listened to what they said and read what they wrote.

"Let your husband lead."

Bobbie and Nancy both believed that their husband was called by God to be their leader, their head, their earthly shepherd. I had no choice about the theme of this book.

Now, back to our halftime conversation. You and I expect that when we step from my office into the locker room there will be some uncertainty and maybe some discouragement on the men's faces. We know that, in this moment, they'll be eager to hear what we have to say. We expect that when we walk into the locker room there will be discouragement and defeat on everyone's face. We know that, in this moment and given the state of this game, they'll be eager to hear what we have to say.

Here we go...

ONE

No Turning Back

---

*No one who puts his hand to the plow and
looks back is fit for the kingdom of God.*

—LUKE 9:62

I first heard the story many years ago as a high school student, and
it still makes me shake my head in wonder. You may remember it
from your world history class. If not, maybe you'll have the same
reaction I did when I first read about it.

In 1518, Hernán Cortés de Monroy y Pizarro, a Spanish colonial
official in Cuba, said good-bye to his wife and ten children and sailed
for Mexico with eleven ships, five hundred soldiers, one hundred sail-
ors, and sixteen horses. His goal was to explore and conquer the empire
of the Aztecs, seizing their vast treasures of gold, silver, and jewels.[1]

The Spaniards landed on the Yucatan Peninsula and made their
way up the coast to Veracruz. When all the provisions had been
brought ashore, Cortés called his men together on the beach for an
announcement. Can you picture these men, tired from the long

journey but eager for conquest, anticipating the riches that they would bring home?

Cortés had other plans. While the men waited on the hot Mexican sand, the commander sent a few volunteers in small boats out to the eleven ships bobbing in the harbor with orders to burn them.

No one knows what Cortés said to his men as the flames consumed their only way back to civilization, but it must have been something like, "There's no turning back, men. I hope you like it here in Mexico, because now it's your home."

It's Good to Have You Along

One day—maybe recently, maybe years ago—you gazed up the church aisle at your fiancée as she prepared to make the long walk to you. The two of you were about to speak your vows and be announced as "husband and wife." Like Cortés's men looking across the water at their burning ships, you realized there's no turning back. This is your bride. Forever. Welcome home.

This is a book about marriage. But I promise not to use cold statistics about the contemporary state of this mysterious bond between a man and a woman. Yes, it's tragic how many marriages are failing, breaking sacred covenant promises along with the hearts of the kids who are caught in the crossfire. But for the moment, these statistics don't matter, because this isn't a book about marriage as an indicator of social wellbeing or decay. It's a book about your own marriage. And my marriage. My goal is to capture your attention as forcefully as Cortés captured his men's on the beach at Veracruz.

Shepherd

I have never experienced an agrarian life, but it's not quite accurate to say that I grew up as a city boy. Our modest split-level was in a neighborhood of single-family homes, with a big, grassy backyard and a driveway for my dad's car. But my roots are in Lancaster County, Pennsylvania, and "our people" were mostly farmers. From many childhood visits to my cousins' places, I saw what it was like to herd cattle and live off the land.

The image I've chosen to represent a man's role in his marriage— a shepherd—might seem mild or even dull. I could have compared a husband to a warrior, an astronaut, a swashbuckler, or a cowboy. Or perhaps, like Cortés, an explorer or conqueror. But other authors have already made these comparisons, appealing to the testosterone-marinated "y" chromosome that sends us onto the field to win, securing the love of a woman by sweeping her up and impressing her with how terrific we can be.

This book, however, is about a challenge greater than any you have ever faced, a challenge that may require the kind of effort you've never attempted before.

The Wind

The story was headlined "Week of extreme weather leaves at least 43 dead across seven states" and was accompanied by photos of homes shredded by an indescribable force that, in a moment, turned sturdy structures into piles of ruin. That force is wind. As I examined those pictures, I wondered what could be more powerful than a tornado. And then I remembered one of my favorite Aesop's fables.

The Wind and the Sun were disputing which was the stronger. Suddenly they saw a traveler coming down the road, and the Sun said: "I see a way to decide our dispute. Whichever of us can cause that traveler to take off his cloak shall be regarded as the stronger. You begin." So the Sun retired behind a cloud, and the Wind began to blow as hard as it could upon the traveler. But the harder he blew the more closely did the traveler wrap his cloak round him, till at last the Wind had to give up in despair. Then the Sun came out and shone in all his glory upon the traveler, who soon found it too hot to walk with his cloak on.[2]

You succeeded in winning your wife. Somehow you persuaded the girl you saw "across a crowded room" eventually to say "I do." Your marriage, however, is not a single game. It's not even a weekend series. It's a lifelong tournament.

YOU WILL WIN YOUR WIFE BY SLIPPING OUT FROM BEHIND A CLOUD AND WARMING HER. INSTEAD OF A CLUB OR A SWORD, YOU NEED A SHEPHERD'S CROOK.

Success in that tournament is more likely with a "sunny" strategy than a "windy" one. You might prefer to win by running the fastest, jumping the highest, or slaying the most dragons. But in your marriage this approach isn't going to work. You will win your wife by slipping out from behind a cloud and warming her. Instead of a club or a sword, you need a shepherd's crook. In this tournament, victory—a happy lifelong marriage—is the result not of conquest or intimidation but of humbly leading.

Stepping Up

On Valentine's Day 2012, my daughter, Missy, and I sat in a consultation room on the surgery floor at Florida's M. D. Anderson Cancer Hospital, meeting with my wife's doctor. The surgery had taken almost seven hours, and we were doing our best to prepare ourselves for the news.

"Bobbie has cancer," the doctor reported evenly. "I did everything I could, but the cancer was everywhere. It was as though someone had taken a handful of sand and thrown it into her body. I removed as much as I could, but because it has spread, getting it all would be impossible." Then the doctor looked straight at me. "Your wife's cancer is Stage IV."

In that moment, after almost forty-two years of marriage, I became a fulltime caregiver. From run-of-the-mill, garden-variety husband to 24/7 au pair—a man nurse. For the next thirty-four months, Bobbie was amazingly, but not surprisingly, valiant. She was usually quite strong, but she needed care, and a new kind of companionship was required of me. Hundreds of visits together to doctors and hospitals and standing by during powerful reactions to trial drugs gave me a chance to understand fully the words I had repeated so blithely at our wedding, "in sickness and in health."

This season of my life became a boot camp, a test track, a proving ground—graduate work in the school of husbanding. Of serving and gently leading. Of shepherding.

In the fall of 2014, I said good-bye to our Bobbie. She was full of joy to the very end, speaking to me and reassuring me of her love, seconds before she slipped into eternity.

Let Your Husband Lead

My assignment as my wife's caregiver during her illness accentuated my role of shepherd, but that role was not new. Years before, Bobbie had determined that the biblical model for husband and wife was a shepherd and a sheep. Week after week, she had challenged the women in her young mothers' Bible study, "Let your husband lead."

For some of those women, Bobbie's advice was hard to take. One, whom I'll call "Beverly," told me, "I have my graduate degree. And because I make plenty of money, I have a full-time nanny so my kids are covered. My husband would love me to stay home with our

I SAW KATHERINE WHISPERING SOMETHING TO BOBBIE AT CHURCH. I DIDN'T HEAR THE CONVERSATION, BUT THE JOY ON BOBBIE'S FACE WAS ENOUGH.

children, but I have too much horsepower to stay parked in the garage." A friend had invited Beverly to "Mrs. Bobbie's Bible study" but had cautioned her about Bobbie's strong admonition to the women in the Bible study to let their husbands lead. Beverly didn't think it was for her, but when her friend persisted she acquiesced. "I'll go once, but that's it. Just once."

By the time she told me all this, Beverly had been attending the Bible study for almost three years, and she had seen for herself how clear the Bible was about letting her husband lead. She added that she and her husband had never been happier in their marriage.

And then there was Katherine, a successful local television news anchorwoman. Her husband, Aaron, had wanted to start their family, but Katherine had other plans. A regular in the Bible study, she had a conversation with Bobbie one day after class, telling her about her situation and perhaps hoping that Bobbie would affirm her decision to delay having babies.

"You're not getting any younger and you don't get any do-overs, Katherine," Bobbie had lovingly said, "If God has given Aaron this desire, pray that God will soften your heart to let Aaron lead."

In a few months, I saw Katherine whispering something to Bobbie at church. I didn't hear the conversation, but the joy on Bobbie's face was enough. Seven months later Katherine's and Aaron's first son was born. Two years later a second boy joined their family. And then, less than a year after Bobbie's death, Katherine gave birth to their third son. And you've never seen a husband and wife more delighted and committed to Jesus and His word

Given the family she came from, the idea of letting her husband lead was new to Bobbie when we married. Her mother, Gerry, didn't have much in the way of formal education but was extremely bright. Her creativity and restless pursuit of the finer things in life made her formidably opportunistic. Growing up in the Depression and watching her own mother feed their boarders more lavishly than she could feed her own children filled Gerry's young heart with a sense of inadequacy and regret. And resolve. Her life would be different.

Bobbie's loveable dentist daddy was a peaceable man but not a leader in their marriage. I never doubted that my mother-in-law loved her husband and he loved her. But in that marriage of a sometimes frustrated woman and a sweet but somewhat fearful man, there was little evidence that she "let him lead."

After decades of tenaciously studying the Bible on her own, Bobbie began to discern the biblical picture of womanhood. As it slowly came into focus, she saw her role and mine in our marriage in a new light. I saw her learning, not without struggles, to offer her obedience to Christ, letting her husband lead.

After Bobbie's death, I married her friend Nancy Leigh DeMoss. First with Bobbie and now with Nancy, the Lord has given me the joy of lovingly and humbly leading.

Scared

Soon after Nancy and I began dating, we talked about the vision for this book. Her ministry, Revive Our Hearts, communicates the Gospel message of "biblical womanhood" through a daily radio program, conferences, and the Internet. In addition to helping women in their relationship with God, Nancy encourages married women to "let your husband lead."

"So what happens to these women when they return home after a conference?" I asked Nancy over dinner at my favorite restaurant. "What if husbands don't fully understand what their wives have just heard?" Acknowledging that this was something she had thought about often, she asked if I thought someone should write a book for these husbands. Even though we were sitting in a lovely Italian cantina, I shot my hand into the air to volunteer like a kid in grade school. "I'd love to write that book," I said.

If your wife believes that God wants her to respect you and embrace your leadership, you're a lucky man. You're a shepherd. You have a special assignment. Congratulations. Now it's time to run. The winning of this race is yours to accomplish. You're the head of your wife and the leader in your home. The shepherd. No one else is available to do this for you.

No one except Jesus.

The author of the letter to the Hebrews really got this one right: "Therefore, since we are surrounded by so great a cloud of witnesses, let us also lay aside every weight, and sin which clings so closely, and let us run with endurance the race that is set before us, looking to Jesus, the founder and perfecter of our faith." (Hebrews 12:1–2)

IF YOUR WIFE BELIEVES THAT GOD WANTS HER TO RESPECT YOU AND EMBRACE YOUR LEADERSHIP, YOU'RE A LUCKY MAN.

If you aren't a bit overwhelmed—scared—by the prospect of being the head of your marriage and the leader in your home, then it's possible that you don't understand the magnitude of the assignment. But if you have the sense that these are bigger shoes than your size ten-and-a-half feet can fill, then God has you exactly where He wants you to be.

Not a New Concept

Ocean surf has always fascinated me. In fact, years ago I purchased a large oil painting of a lighthouse standing guard over an expanse of waves breaking on the shore. The turquoise of the water just inside the concave swells about to crash into the sand beautifully captures the scene.

If I could add something to the painting, it would be a big rock in the water about a hundred feet from the shore, because that's how I think of the timelessness of God's plan for marriage. When the tide is in, only the top portion of the rock is visible. But after the tide goes out, the rock, which we now see in its entirety, looks like it has moved. It hasn't moved, of course. Only the tide has. The rock is where it always was.

A couple of centuries ago, a book about the need for husbands to lead would not have sold many copies. No one needed to be reminded. Charles Spurgeon, the nineteenth-century "Prince of Preachers," wrote:

> When God becomes a husband, he undertakes to do a husband's part. When he says, "Your Creator is your husband," you may rest assured that he does not take up the relationship without assuming (well, I must say it) all the responsibilities, which belong to a husband. God's part is to nourish, to cherish, to shield, to protect, and to bless those with whom he condescends, in infinite mercy, to enter into the union of marriage. When the Lord Jesus Christ became the husband of his church, he felt that he had an obligation and commitment to us, and inasmuch as there were debts incurred, he paid them.[3]

So this idea that a husband is the head of his wife as Christ is the head of His church has been in play for a long time. I'm taking this position humbly and without apology, and I'm going to do my best to bring you along. You are the head of your wife. No one can take your place. You're like a running back to whom the quarterback has just handed off the football. You were born to carry it. And, to tell you the truth, the next few steps could be fraught with danger.

So how in the world are you going to do this well?

Inadequate

Webb Simpson was walking down the fairway of the seventeenth hole at the 2012 U.S. Open at the Olympia near San Francisco. This was a short—for the pros—par five, measuring just 505 yards. Holding a one-stroke lead, with a solid opportunity for a birdie, Webb knew that the next twenty-five minutes would be the most important of his career to that date.

The pressure mounting, Webb stopped walking, closed his eyes, and bowed his head ever so slightly. His caddy, Paul Tesori, concerned, stopped too. "What's up, Webb?" he asked, unable to hide the worry in his voice. After a pause, Webb said, "I'm praying."

"Praying?" Paul wondered, "That you'll hold on and win this thing?" Webb didn't speak for a moment. Then he turned and said, "No, not that. I'm praying because I don't know if I can do this. But, whatever happens, what I really care about is that God is honored."

In recalling the moment, Webb says the best way to describe how he felt at the moment was "strangely unqualified." Within a few strokes of walking onto a world stage and lifting a trophy engraved with the names of Jones, Trevino, Nicklaus, Watson, and Woods, he felt an overwhelming sense of inadequacy, humility and fear filling his heart. As though he was a spectator rather than the player, like a frightened sheep bleating for his shepherd to carry him, Webb called on a God Who was listening carefully to his cry for help. And Webb's Shepherd *was* listening. And caring. And answering.

This is you. This is me. The assignment of leading our marriage with love and grace is, to say the least, a daunting one. *What if I fail? What if I disappoint my wife and she loses confidence in me?* This, my friend, is exactly where God wants you to be. Overwhelmed. Depending on Him Who is more than adequate. Being a shepherd is a big deal. Doing it on your own isn't going to work out so well.

And, to make it even more intimidating, there's no turning back. Like Cortés's men on the beach at Veracruz, you're home for good.

So, take a deep breath. Let's do this. Together.

TWO

SHEEP

During our engagement, Nancy and I visited the astoundingly beautiful Jackson Hole, Wyoming. A thoroughly chaperoned trip with two married couples, they suggested that we go to the rodeo. Having grown up in Chicago's suburbs, where a visit to the A&W root beer stand was considered an adventure, this would be my first in-person exposure to such a thing.

The evening was cool for August, so we bundled up. Watching cowboys attempt to ride bucking broncos and steers that were, for some reason, really ticked off, was remarkable. To hang on for even a few seconds, you've got to be an exceptional athlete and wildly daring—and these guys were. But only a few stayed on board for long. We all agreed that the animals won the evening. The cowboys took it in the shorts.

We pictured the horses and cattle in the clubhouse after the event, hoof bumping each other in celebration.

Halfway through the rodeo, it was the kids' turn. The announcer invited all children to come to the center of the arena, and at least three hundred of the little ones responded. I had no idea what was coming next.

WE ALL AGREED THAT THE ANIMALS WON THE EVENING. THE COWBOYS TOOK IT IN THE SHORTS.

The announcer informed us that "we're going to play a game tonight of 'catching sheep.'" And there were prizes for each of the kids who successfully wrapped one up. So I'm picturing little, sweet, woolly lambs and hoping the kids don't hurt them.

Presently three sheep were released into the crowd of children—not lambs but full-size sheep. They were huge compared with the kids who gleefully chased them around the arena, much larger than even the oldest child out there. Raucous music blasted from the speakers. It was pandemonium.

"This is not going to end well, "I said to Nancy. Looking at either end of the field, I expected to see paramedic trucks in waiting, as they do for football games. "These kids are going to get hurt."

The children swarmed the sheep, which cowered in fear and then stampeded in retreat. They clearly had no idea how much larger they were than the children, nor did they have any plans to do them any harm. It took about ten minutes for a victorious kid to wrap himself around the neck of each frightened and confused animal. The three winners were presented gift certificates to the rodeo merchandise booth, and the color began to return to my face.

Whom Are You Calling a Sheep?

I had seen sheep from a distance, languidly grazing in grassy pastures along the interstate, but that night at the rodeo was my first close-up exposure to these animals. My first impression? Not great.

I had already decided to write a book called *Like the Shepherd* and had begun to distribute a proposal. The simile in the title set the stage for husbands to embrace their role as shepherd in their marriage. So far, so good. The problem was that, if the husband is a shepherd, his wife must be a *sheep*. Let's just say there was not a lot of enthusiasm for that idea among the publishers I was talking to.

And who can blame them? Sheep aren't terribly impressive, as I learned at the rodeo. But you don't need to be a scholar of Scripture to realize that the Bible is filled with sheep imagery. If your wife is a sheep, she's in good company.

"My sheep were scattered; they wandered over all the mountains and on every high hill. My sheep were scattered over all the face of the earth, with none to search or seek for them." (Ezekiel 34:6)

"All we like sheep have gone astray; we have turned—every one—to his own way.... " (Isaiah 53:6)

"When [Jesus] saw the crowds, he had compassion for them, because they were harassed and helpless, like sheep without a shepherd." (Matthew 9:36)

"And Jesus, when He came out, saw a great multitude and was moved with compassion for them, because they were like sheep not having a shepherd. So He began to teach them many things." (Mark 6:34)

THE CHILDREN SWARMED THE SHEEP, WHICH COWERED IN FEAR AND THEN STAMPEDED IN RETREAT.

Did you notice that in each of these verses, sheep—representing you and me—are in some kind of trouble? I noticed that, too. But we're not the only ones who are compared to sheep. Referring to the Messiah that is to come, Isaiah writes, "He was oppressed, and he was afflicted, yet he opened not his mouth; like a lamb that is led to the slaughter, and like a sheep that before its shearers is silent, so he opened not his mouth." (53:7)

AND WHO CAN BLAME THEM? SHEEP AREN'T TERRIBLY IMPRESSIVE, AS I LEARNED AT THE RODEO. BUT YOU DON'T NEED TO BE A SCHOLAR OF SCRIPTURE TO REALIZE THAT THE BIBLE IS FILLED WITH SHEEP IMAGERY.

If ever there was a graphic depiction of an infinite God's "stooping" to become a mortal, this is it. Given what we now know about sheep, it's breathtaking to realize that the God Who spoke these creatures into existence with His voice identified Himself with them. And it's even more breathtaking the more you know about sheep. People who really know sheep say that they are slow to learn, demanding, stubborn, prone to stray, unpredictable, and restless.[1]

Prone to Wander

Several years ago, friends of mine went on a camping trip 150 miles from their home. And they took their collie, Trooper, along. Three days later, as they were getting ready to return, they noticed that Trooper was missing. After an all-out search, including inquiries at the ranger station, failed to turn up the dog, they reluctantly headed home without Trooper. A week later—you know where this is going, don't you?—Trooper came trotting down their long driveway. He looked like he had made a 150-mile journey by himself, but he was alive. If Trooper had been a sheep, he'd still be out there, maybe not even aware that he was lost.

The people that Jesus preached to knew sheep. One tasty tuft of delicious grass here and then another over there... and then another... and another... and soon the foolish critter is out of range. The parable of the lost sheep (Luke 15:3–7) made perfect sense to them.

When I compare someone to a sheep, I realize just how shocking that comparison is. The idea that each of us—you, me, our wives—is a sheep is pretty radical. The Bible says it's true.

That's why we all need a Shepherd.

The Call to Keeping
Her Heart Full

Not long ago I read a blog post from a New York Times best selling author named Jane Green. The title of her post caught my eye: "Why the Forty-Something Woman is at Risk for an Affair."

As I read the short article I was gripped with the challenge that you and I face when it comes to loving and leading our wives. The relentless, ongoing task of keeping her heart tender toward us long after we win her heart and marry her is no small challenge.

Green confessed: "…I did a book event with a young, handsome author, who exchanged email addresses with me, and proceeded to indulge me with a series of gently flirtatious emails, which was both exciting and unsettling. It had little to do with him, but to do with me, and my growing feelings of invisibility, and the addictive quality of someone, *anyone*, actually noticing me, paying me attention, making me feel beautiful again."

The author had been fascinated with what she called a "worrying trend."

It seemed that some women she knew—wives who had appeared to be happily married—suddenly announced they had been unhappy for years, and could no longer continue with this sham of a marriage.

She continued: "Recently I asked one of these women who lives in my town and left her husband, a woman who describes her now-ex-husband as the love of her life, why she had an affair. 'I was bored', she said, and as callous as that may be, I understood what she meant."

GIVEN WHAT WE NOW KNOW ABOUT SHEEP, IT'S BREATHTAKING TO REALIZE THAT THE GOD WHO SPOKE THESE CREATURES INTO EXISTENCE WITH HIS VOICE IDENTIFIED HIMSELF WITH THEM.

THE RELENTLESS, ONGOING TASK OF KEEPING HER HEART TENDER TOWARD US LONG AFTER WE WIN HER HEART AND MARRY HER IS NO SMALL CHALLENGE.

"However wonderful our marriages are, however wonderful our husbands, when children are waking us up, repeatedly, at 5am, when every night is spent figuring out what to make for dinner, when mornings are spent shoveling laundry into the dryer and remembering the days when you actually had time to iron, it's very difficult to remember the passion and lust that brought you and your husband together.

"When your weekends are not spent holding hands over a candlelit dinner, but instead ferrying four children around from basketball game to basketball game, to play-date, to ice skating, to birthday party, it's very difficult to remember the importance of appreciating your spouse, or indeed to find the time to remember to be kind, to pay attention to each other, to make each other feel loved.

"Marriage becomes pots and pans. At first you're distracted by those tiny children, but all of a sudden you're in your forties, your kids are in grade school, you're no longer needed in the way you once were, and you start to feel irrelevant." [2]

If you have only been married for a few months or a few years, what you've just read could seem outrageous. You meant what you said about "till death do us part." And you're sure that your bride meant it, too. But if your anniversaries are in the double digits, you may get a queasy feeling considering the implications. Perhaps you're wondering about the likelihood that a deep sense of loss and isolation could happen to your wife. And, by association, to you.

But I can't control what my wife is thinking, you may be saying. And of course, you're right. You and I have no way to either know or supervise the wanderings of her heart.

How well I remember the Glen Campbell song that hit the charts during my college years. Actually, I was gripped by the song about an aging wife whose meandering heart was quietly fantasizing about her life. Her reverie. Her plight.

It's not an overstatement to tell you that, even at a young age, the words Campbell sang in "Dreams of the Everyday Housewife" haunted me. What if this happens to my wife? What if she scans old photos, old memories, and feels a sense of loneliness? Or regret. What if, after years of marriage, she decides that she really doesn't love me and so, for the sake of the kids or just to endure, she rides out the rest of her life wishing for something—someone other than me?

The call to lead your wife with love and grace is the call to be the kind of husband that draws your wife in, a tenderness and humble leadership that serves her well. It's the kind of confidence and humility that surgically dispels her anxieties and fears. It's "headship" that provides a safe place for her to moor her heart.

As her husband, you have the opportunity to speak words into her life that remind her that you still value her, words that confirm that she still has the kind of beauty that drew you to her in the first place. You lavish her with words that nurture and water any dryness in her heart that comes from years of routine and sometimes thankless work. Day by day, you resolve to not grow weary of "giving yourself for her."

PERHAPS YOU'RE WONDERING ABOUT THE LIKELIHOOD THAT A DEEP SENSE OF LOSS AND ISOLATION COULD HAPPEN TO YOUR WIFE.

This is the kind of leader that I believe the Bible compels you and me to be.

What's in a Name?

In 2002, I was introduced to Nancy Leigh DeMoss. I first heard her name from Dr. Henry Blackaby, the author of the popular *Experiencing God* Bible study and a client of my literary representation firm. An admirer of Nancy's writing and ministry, he was certain that I should

> THE CALL TO LEAD YOUR WIFE WITH LOVE AND GRACE IS THE CALL TO BE THE KIND OF HUSBAND THAT DRAWS YOUR WIFE IN, A TENDERNESS AND HUMBLE LEADERSHIP THAT SERVES HER WELL.

sign Nancy as a client, as I eventually did. It was good to learn to know this biblically-grounded, bright, smart, faithful, capable thinker, writer, and speaker. Hers was a well-known and highly respected name in women's ministry in America and around the world. Guarded by an unequivocal call to ministry and virtue, neither one of us could have even imagined any kind a friendship that would have crossed the line of propriety. Our settings were never one-on-one. I was in a wonderful marriage and Nancy was committed to singleness.

Soon Nancy met Bobbie, and the two became friends.

Nancy's ministry grew, and a couple of years later one of her colleagues took over the contract negotiating and marketing consulting that I had been handling. I knew that I'd miss working with Nancy and her ministry colleagues, but it was a sensible business decision for them. Except for a few gifts and hand-written notes of encouragement to Bobbie during her cancer journey, I essentially lost track of Nancy's life.

Fast forward to late 2014. Bobbie had stepped into heaven after a two-and-a-half year battle with cancer. After a "chance" meeting with Nancy's brother, Mark, whom I had known for many years, I reached out to Nancy in an email. Five months later I proposed to her.

Not long after announcing our engagement, Nancy and her team asked my firm to represent her book writing again. Stepping back into this professional role was sweet, to be sure. And in telling this story, Nancy likes to say, "I may be the only writer to hire, fire, and marry her agent."[3]

In June 2015, Nancy and her colleagues and my colleagues and I had our first professional meeting in more than a dozen years. In publishing, as in many other businesses, effective branding is critical, so the issue of Nancy's name was raised. For the millions of women who had purchased one of her books and the countless people in her radio audience, Nancy Leigh DeMoss—"NLD," as we called the brand—meant something important. I remember saying, "After we're married, I think you should keep NLD as your public pen name."

A month before our wedding, Nancy and I met with her senior leadership team. This time the only topic of conversation was the NLD brand. We had to consider donor letters, radio, and publications. Experts weighed in on what name Nancy should use on her books. There were strong feelings on both sides—civil, but strong.

In private life she would be Nancy Wolgemuth. That was never in question. But the issue was the public presentation. The brand. Were we ready to ask folks who had been loyal NLD followers for decades to make this change? Nancy and I prayed about this decision. It was much bigger than the two of us, and so I led our conversation to the Throne, to the Good Shepherd. His wisdom would be essential.

Two weeks before our wedding, Nancy and I sat in my car in her driveway, praying about the decision once again. After a few minutes of silence, Nancy spoke. "We have talked about this with people we trust. And we've prayed about it many times." She paused. "The final decision is yours to make, Robert. You're my shepherd. I trust the Lord to work through your leadership on this."

The condo where I was living was thirty minutes from Nancy's house. The drive went by in a blur. The good news was that my wife-to-be trusted me. She had taken the necessary time to be a part of the journey.

> "I MAY BE THE ONLY WRITER TO HIRE, FIRE, AND MARRY HER AGENT."

The bad news was that the final decision, which had to be made, was my responsibility. For NLD's colleagues, constituents, and corporate associates, I would be held responsible for the outcome.

To say that the next twenty hours were intense would be an understatement. I spent much of the time on my knees in prayer. Although I had done my best to gather all the information I could, I knew it wasn't enough. It would never be enough. There was much that a finite mind could not know or forecast.

So I turned to the Good Shepherd. I asked Him for wisdom. I asked Him to tell me what I could not hear. To show me what I could not see. I asked Him to lead me.

NDW

The next morning the decision about her name would be made.

I arrived at her house around ten o'clock, heading first to the kitchen for a cup of coffee and then to the living room, where Nancy was waiting with a hug. We sat down where I had proposed marriage six months before. We prayed first, then we read from the Scripture together, and we prayed again. Then we talked about the process of the past few days and the importance of following our Shepherd's lead in getting this right.

I TURNED TO LOOK INTO THE FACE OF THE WOMAN WHO WOULD, IN TWO WEEKS, BE MY WIFE. HER EYES WELLED UP WITH TEARS, AS DID MINE.

Almost an hour later, Nancy asked, "Well, Robert, what do you think I should do about my name?"

I had invited and welcomed my Shepherd's leading. I had promised to be a good and faithful servant, a sheep who follows well. I felt resolved. "I believe your name needs to be Nancy DeMoss Wolgemuth—on everything," I said.

There was a moment of silence. Nancy had asked me to lead. And I knew that she trusted the Lord with the outcome of the decision. But I also knew that she had to be considering the cascade of implications, not to mention making phone calls to some important people in her life who would disagree with the decision.

I turned to look into the face of the woman who would, in two weeks, be my wife. Her eyes welled up with tears, as did mine.

"Okay," she said simply. "It's NDW."

Riding on the Point

Over the years, I have often referred to what I believe were the most important six weeks in my young adult life. In the spring of 1968, I, along with about forty men friends, set out on a bicycle trip from San Francisco to New York City. And for the next forty-two days, we rode eastward, from dawn to dusk, every single day—four thousand miles under our own power. Since we traveled on highways that were also occupied by cars and trucks, we rode in groups of five or six riders spaced a mile apart. Traveling in these packs enabled motor vehicles to pass us safely.

It wasn't until this experience that I learned how mighty a headwind could be when you're on a bicycle. And even though prevailing winds are supposed to blow from west to east, there were times when the wind blew directly into our faces.

The rider leading each small pack of five or six men had the taxing responsibility of opening a wedge of wind in which the riders behind him could ride. The leader also called out potential hazards on the highway. "Rock on the left," he'd holler, or, "rubber on the right" (referring to separated tire treads on the roadside).

On a blue, twenty-eight-pound Schwinn Super Sport, I learned about leadership. The hard work, the dangers, the responsibility. These lessons meant even more to me when, two years later, I became a husband. They were lessons I did not forget.

I was launching out on a marriage and not a cross-country bike trip. But what I had learned about effectively and soberly leading a little pack of riders, giving them confidence as they rode in my wake, had the potential of giving my wife that same sense of feeling safe. And certain. And strong.

If I would resolve to be a leader that my wife respected and admired, a man whose tender and transparent life she emulated, a husband that was the kind of person she actually wanted to be herself, my wife could willingly consent to join me on the journey.

She just might lovingly follow.

THREE

"AND WHAT DOES YOUR HUSBAND DO?"

You and I share some shepherding history. It's true.

It was about four thousand years ago that the Egyptian pharaoh invited Jacob and his family to leave the famine in Canaan and move to his country. Because of the shrewd leadership of Joseph, Jacob's eleventh son, who as a youth had been sold by his jealous brothers into slavery, Egypt was the land of plenty. Canaan, not so much.

When Joseph's brothers arrived in Egypt, they were given an audience with the pharaoh himself. "What is your occupation," he asked them, no doubt wondering where this huge family should settle. "Your servants are shepherds, as our fathers were," they answered (Genesis 47:3).

Even if you and I are not Jewish, our spiritual lineage by way of the Old Testament includes plenty of career shepherds. These men understood what it meant to carefully tend to the needs of their flocks. In fact, one of the most remarkable features of the account of the migration of Jacob's family from Canaan to Egypt is that sheep also made the journey. On hoof. All four hundred miles over challenging terrain filled with thieves and wild animals looking for fresh mutton for dinner.

Moving

Early in the summer of 2015, Nancy and I—mostly Nancy—were making plans for our wedding in November. We were talking through housing options. My home was in Orlando, hers in southwestern Michigan. We had decided to sell my house and find a condominium in Florida, thinking that we'd spend the warm half the year in the north and cold half in the south.

Happily, we had a contract on the Florida house in less than thirty days, and I started looking at condos. With Nancy living a thousand miles away, I did my best to report my findings and observations with each visit to a potential new high-rise home. One Friday evening, as I was giving her the real estate update, a thought swept over me. I did not mention it immediately, continuing with my descriptions of condos, but it grew more and more pronounced, and eventually I could not hold it back.

"Let's not buy a condo in Florida," I blurted out. "I think the Lord wants me to move to Michigan. Full time."

I knew that doing this would make the next few months far less stressful for my bride-to-be. Except for making room for a husband in her home—no small task for a fifty-seven-year-old never-married woman—there would be a minimal amount of adjustments required. On the other hand—and Nancy knew this full well—my life would become chaotic. It's challenging enough to move from one house to another, but I would be distributing my belongings among four locations—Nancy's home, my two daughters' homes, and a new location for my business, which had been headquartered in the Florida house. There was a lot of work ahead.

"THANK YOU FOR THE HONOR OF BEING YOUR SHEPHERD," I FINALLY SAID. "THANK YOU FOR THE PURE JOY OF LEADING."

Since I was on a video call with Nancy, I could see her face as I was describing the plan. Her eyes widened with a sense of wonder. After a long pause, she said, "You would do that for me?" I felt a lump forming in my throat. I knew that Nancy understood what the next few months would be like for me. I could tell that she was feeling the emotion of it as well.

At that moment, a passage from Scripture came to mind. It's from the Apostle Paul's description of Christ's love for His people, the church. It's an exhortation to husbands like you and me, who are eager to be good shepherds in our marriages.

"I have five words for you," I said to my fiancée with a smile.

"Just five?" she returned wearing a smile I love so much.

"Yes...just five." I paused. Nancy waited. "And gave Himself for her," I said, quoting Ephesians 5:25. The emotion that had made a lump in my throat traveled north, and tears welled up in my eyes.

Nancy knew the Bible verse well. She understood its implications. "You would do this for me?" she repeated. I nodded. Spoken words would need to wait for a minute or two. "Thank you for the honor of being your shepherd," I finally said. "Thank you for the pure joy of leading."

Savior like a Shepherd Lead Us

The model for us in our marriages is Jesus' relationship to us. He is our Shepherd. He is our Leader.

About seven hundred years before the birth of Jesus, Isaiah prophesied about the coming Messiah, "He will tend his flock like a shepherd; he will gather the lambs in his arms; he will carry them in his bosom, and gently lead those that are with young." (Isaiah 40:11)

And yes, Jesus' shepherding love is so vast that He was willing to give his life for us. This Shepherd is our Savior. "I am the good Shepherd. The good shepherd lays down His life for His sheep." (John 10:11)

When you and your wife were dating, you may have had a love song that you picked out together. You called it "our song." A few weeks after announcing our engagement, Nancy and I went to dinner not far from her home. She had "some secret, pre-wedding shopping" to do and asked me to go ahead to the restaurant, where she would join me shortly.

As I was waiting, a man began to play a piano in the corner. His repertoire seemed to be old love songs. A romantic from my teenage years, I recognized nearly every one of them. "This is perfect," I thought to myself. "Wait till Nancy is here. She'll love it." She arrived soon, and after she was settled, I said, "Listen to the piano music. The guy is playing love songs from the seventies and eighties. And even though a few patrons have come into the place, he's playing just for us." Nancy took my hand and smiled right back.

As he played through old favorites like "You Are the Sunshine of My Life" and "Misty," I'd softly croon a line or two of the song. First Nancy grinned. And then, with a squeeze of my hand and a sparkle in her eyes, my fiancée confessed, "None of these songs is familiar. I don't know any of them. I've never been in love before."

"That's okay," I said as I grinned back. "You're in love now." I kept singing.

After our dinner, Nancy told me that it had been fun to hear those old songs, but as we talked in the car on the way back to her house, we came to the conclusion that no music is more romantic than hymns. As crazy—and possibly nerdy—as that sounds, Nancy and I realized that nothing draws our hearts to each other as powerfully as the awareness of our heavenly Father's love and presence.

That night we picked "our song," From the beginning of our courtship, Nancy and I quoted Dorothy A. Thrupp's "Savior, Like a Shepherd Lead Us" many times in emails and text messages and when we were together.

Savior, like a Shepherd lead us,

Much we need Thy tender care;

In Thy pleasant pastures feed us,

For our use Thy folds prepare.

And so the image of a shepherd and his sheep became the theme of our friendship. Our love. Our future. Together.

Shepherdless Sheep

I need a shepherd. You need a shepherd. Your wife needs a shepherd. But there's something even more important than that. If our Shepherd is going to lead us, we must learn how to be His lambs.

Take a moment to let that settle in. We can have fun describing these critters. We can smile at their questionable hygiene, vulnerability, and propensity to wander off. But if we want the Shepherd to care for us, we have no choice but to learn how to be sheep. And, trust me on this one—sheep without a shepherd are a sorry lot.

IF OUR SHEPHERD IS GOING TO LEAD US, WE MUST LEARN HOW TO BE HIS LAMBS.

If you have any doubts about that, I refer you to Shrek, a ewe whose plight aroused the sympathy of millions when her picture was posted on Facebook. Shrek seems to have hidden for six years in a cave, where she had no shepherd—no one to protect her, to lead her, or to *shear* her. The average sheep delivers ten to fifteen pounds of wool with a single shearing. But after Shrek emerged from her cave, her shearing produced sixty pounds of wool.

Just Between You and Me

As I have acknowledged, this "shepherd" concept may take you a while to get used to. It took me a while. But one hundred years ago, no one would have bothered to write this book. Not that every man did this well, but it was taken for granted that a husband was supposed to lead his marriage with love and grace. But this isn't a hundred years ago, and the husband's leadership in marriage is now seen as controversial, politically incorrect—even anathema.

The first hint I got that relations between the sexes were going awry came when I was a callow teenager living in Wheaton, Illinois, running an errand for my dad at Soukup's Hardware store in our home town. As I approached the entrance, I saw a woman coming from the opposite direction. We arrived at the door simultaneously, and I instinctively reached out and opened it for her. She stopped and looked at me with withering disdain. I did not understand and continued to hold the door. She did not move. I smiled and nodded toward the open door, thinking she might not realize that I was holding it for her. As it turned out, she understood perfectly well.

And then she spoke. With the equanimity of an angry junior high assistant principal, she said through clenched teeth, "Well, young man, you don't understand. Haven't you ever heard of women's liberation?" At that, she glared at me in anger, tossed her head back, and proceeded through the open door.

I was utterly shocked. And she was right—I hadn't heard much about women's liberation, so I didn't understand. I was just chagrined and embarrassed. Perhaps that's what the woman intended. Or maybe she had been pushed around too long by men who treated her rudely. Maybe just because I was a man—quite a young one—I deserved this.

This incident aroused many emotions, which lingered for several days, but one feeling was most pronounced. It would plague my relations with women for many years—including my relationship with my wife. That feeling was *uncertainty.*

IT WOULD PLAGUE MY RELATIONS WITH WOMEN FOR MANY YEARS—INCLUDING MY RELATIONSHIP WITH MY WIFE. THAT FEELING WAS *UNCERTAINTY.*

The Seesaw

It was the most dangerous contraption on the playground. I put this in the past tense because I'm pretty sure they've all been expunged by some watchdog government agency. And for good reason. This time the bureaucrats got it right. When I was a kid in elementary school, there were three—count them, three—of these on the playground. Of course, I'm referring to the seesaw. Or, as we used to call it, the "teeter-totter." The name makes the thing sound friendly and harmless. It wasn't.

Of all the equipment in the playground, the seesaw—a twelve-foot board fastened in the middle to a horizontal pipe about eighteen inches from the ground—was probably the least expensive. As anyone who ever played on one knows, the operation of a seesaw depends on trust. The rider on the elevated end is completely vulnerable. If the child on the lower end suddenly dismounts, his friend on the high end will suffer an unpleasant crash landing.

Now let's imagine that you and your wife are sitting on a seesaw. You're on one end and she's on the other. You're in sweet balance. And then you begin the dance.

You push off and the motion lifts you off the ground. Your wife descends. Then, while you're in the air, she pushes off, lifting herself off the ground and lowering you. You repeat this several times, and your smiles indicate that all is well. You love her. She loves you. You are trustworthy. She trusts you. You serve her. She respects you. You lead her. Because you have a shepherd's heart and not a cowboy's, she graciously and joyfully surrenders to your leadership. You do not push or drive, you lead. Her submission inspires you to love, serve, and lead with growing confidence, which in turn inspires confidence in her.

At this point, however, you might be thinking, "I'm glad you have a happy seesaw marriage. But my wife is more like the woman you encountered at the hardware store. For her, 'submission' means being dragged around by the hair by a caveman." What if your wife is resolved to challenge you at every level, to turn your marriage into a contest of wills? What if every conversation, every decision, every conflict is something to win or something to lose?

Shhhhh . . .

If this describes you, may I suggest a special approach? Under normal circumstances, I'm a big fan of full disclosure in marriage. Secrets can be like a small pebble in your shoe. But this time, I'm going to suggest a different strategy. Do not tell her what I've just said. Say nothing about the seesaw. Keep all of this under the cloak of silence and mystery. For now.

Once upon a time there was an angry man who intended to file for divorce. Full of spite, he confided to a friend how he would make the experience as painful as possible for his wife. "For the next thirty days," he said, "I'm going to do everything I can to serve my wife. I'm going to speak loving words to her and look for ways to lavish her with kindness." After a month of such treatment, he would serve her with divorce papers. "Imagine how, after my being so nice to her, this will break her heart!"

Thirty days later, this man met again with his friend. "Well?" the friend asked. "How did it go? Did you treat her as you said you were going to? And did you serve her the papers? Was she crushed?"

"Are you kidding me," the man replied. "I am having the time of my life. My wife is amazing. Divorce her? Are you serious? I have never been more in love than I am today."

If you treat your wife as the husband in that story treated his—without the sinister motivation, of course—you may be surprised by the results. It's what Alex and Stephen Kendrick explain in their book *The Love Dare* and my wife, Nancy, describes in her *30-Day Husband Encouragement Challenge*. You will be giving your wife a taste of what it's like to be shepherded. Just like Jesus, you're going to love her "as you love your own body" (Ephesians 5:25–28). Never underestimate the power of those five words of Paul's—"and gave Himself for her." Because of your humble spirit, your wife will be ready to hear you. To love you. To embrace your plan. In the next chapter, I'll unpack this in more detail.

But remember, you cannot do this on your own. You're going to hear me say this over and over again, so I apologize for repeating myself. But your ability to be a shepherd depends on your experience of being shepherded…by the Good Shepherd.

Stay with me on this journey. I hope you and your wife will be glad you did.

FOUR

HAVING EVERYTHING

The Lord is my shepherd, I shall not want.

—PSALM 23:1

I n my forty-five years of teaching Sunday school, I almost always based the first lesson of the new year on a passage from the epistle to the Hebrews. As you might expect, that passage is now deeply engraved on my heart:

> Therefore, since we are surrounded by so great a cloud of witnesses, let us also lay aside every weight, and sin which clings so closely, and let us run with endurance the race that is set before us, looking to Jesus, the founder and perfecter of our faith, who for the joy that was set before him endured the cross, despising the shame, and is seated at the right hand of the throne of God. (Hebrews 12:1–2)

In the race of life, Jesus leads. You and I follow. He sets the pace. We learn from Him.

Let's be honest: This sounds pretty confining, doesn't it? By nature, we're adventurers. Our hearts pound with expectation when we are introduced to the open range. We embrace the chance to run free. But being told to follow in the footsteps of the runner—who is also a shepherd—just a few strides ahead of us could sound like some kind of prison sentence.

An incorrigible entrepreneur since childhood, I understand this feeling. Who wants to be a follower?

The Real Challenge of the Good News

When I finished college, I worked for a while as a youth minister, and fifty years later, I'm still in contact with some of the young men and women I knew then. But it wasn't what I taught these teenagers that's memorable, it's what I learned from them.

Most of my conversations with these kids were about the life choices they faced. I did my best to lean in lovingly on these easily distracted young people about the seriousness of the choices they were making—a seriousness we usually don't appreciate until we're older.

Presenting the Gospel to these kids in a way that was compelling and inspiring was an enormous challenge. At first, I tried something that sounded like a motivational speech: "Hey, why not go ahead and receive Jesus as your Savior, your Shepherd? He'll make you even better than you already are. You have nothing to lose. Why wouldn't you believe in Jesus? He'll make you great."

But this approach did not work because it wasn't true. The message of the Gospel is this: You and I are sheep. We need a shepherd. We may long for the fence-less open field, but without Someone to show us the way, we're completely lost. So this became my message to these teenagers. But the look on their faces said "This sounds like I am giving up my ability to choose!"

And so, as every teacher confronted with hard questions does, I dug deeper, and I found something I still have not forgotten. I couldn't put it better than the plain-spoken Apostle Paul, so I paraphrased the sixth chapter of his letter to the Romans. "You are

THE MOST IMPORTANT CHOICE YOU'LL EVER MAKE IS THE SELECTION OF YOUR MASTER

going to make choices," I told those kids, "but the most important choice you'll ever make is the selection of your master. In fact, every person you know has embraced something or someone who makes the call. A master who controls your every move. Every decision. Actually, this isn't the most important choice you make, it's the *only* choice you *get* to make."

In other words, we are destined to be sheep. As independent as we think we are, we are followers. Given our human condition, our choices—our passions—lead us. These passions take control. They are our shepherds. Just ask someone who's in addiction recovery. Our choice in life—our only real choice—is the selection of our master, our shepherd.

If that's true, then the opening line of the twenty-third Psalm— "The Lord is my Shepherd"—presents us with the breathtaking opportunity to choose Jesus as our Leader, our Shepherd. Imagine, selecting the Creator of the universe to lead us. Can we do better than this?

I Shall Not Want

For many years, my extended family—almost one hundred strong, with my five siblings and their children and grandchildren— has been singing Ralph Carmichael's setting of Psalm 23 whenever

SOME GUY IN A
BATHROBE AND FLIP-
FLOPS WITH A CROOKED
STICK IN HIS HAND
GIVES US EVERYTHING
WE NEED. SERIOUSLY?
THIS IS FOOLISHNESS.

we're together for a wedding, a funeral, or a reunion. There's just something about the way the harmonies feather themselves perfectly with the various voices in our clan.

"The Lord is my shepherd, I shall not want" is one of the most familiar sentences in Scripture. But perhaps for that reason, this beloved verse is often ignored. We've heard it so often that we pay no attention to it. But Carmichael's musical setting uses the paraphrase of the Living Bible—"Because the Lord is my Shepherd, I have everything that I need"—which captures what the Psalmist is saying in a particularly powerful way.

It wasn't until a few years ago that I was struck by this verse, especially the word "everything." That's a remarkable promise, don't you think? *Everything?* Yes, everything. As a result of my relationship with my very own Shepherd, there isn't anything I need that I don't have. I have it all.

To modern ears, however, this sounds awfully naïve. It's saying that some guy in a bathrobe and flip-flops with a crooked stick in his hand gives us everything we need. Seriously? This is foolishness. We have proposals to finish, ends to meet, apps to download, major projects that are waiting, relationships struggling to survive. And then there is the stuff we long for that we don't own. Every year more than two hundred billion dollars is spent on advertising. The ads show up on billboards and as banner ads on every website we visit. In fact, our computers and smart phones know us by our desires, offering products that match our demonstrated interests. The message is clear. You and I don't have everything we need. We're missing out on something.

Actually, I have a confession. It's going to make me feel good to get this off my chest. For most of my professional career I have been guilty of encouraging people to separate themselves from their money to buy what I'm promoting. It's the purpose of marketing. It's the reason all these dollars are being spent. Here's the message: We live with plenty of wants...like we *don't* have everything we need. Not even close. In our minds, there are lots of things we don't have—things, tangible and intangible, we long for.

But according to Psalm 23, King David chose a Shepherd. His job description can be summarized in a single word: *Leader*. And ours can too: *follower*. When we follow our Good Shepherd—our Leader—our desires are supposed to be satisfied. "Our cup runs over."

Your Wife Is a Lamb

"Wives, submit to your own husbands, as to the Lord. For the husband is the head of the wife even as Christ is the head of the church, his body, and is himself its Savior. Now as the church submits to Christ, so also wives should submit in everything to their husbands." (Ephesians 5:22–24)

This may be the most controversial—and misunderstood—passage in the entire Bible, provoking innumerable schisms. But it shouldn't be so. Many years ago, on a flight from Chicago to Orlando, I sat next to a woman who was so deeply engrossed in a book that she never looked up. I had a lot of work to do, so I was not unhappy with the quiet arrangement. But as we approached Orlando, she closed her book and said hello. I returned her greeting and for the next few minutes we talked.

This woman was inquisitive, and I could tell she was smart. Even after a few partially answered questions from me, I learned very little about her besides her name. But Edith seemed intensely interested in what I did—so much so that I wondered if she had peeked at the correspondence I had been conducting on my laptop. "Are you a Christian?" Edith asked, the tone of her voice letting me know that if I were to answer in the affirmative, I was in for a battle.

"Yes," I said. "I'm a Christian." Even though our flight was almost over, Edith peppered me with more questions, eventually getting to the point: "I'll bet you're one of those fundamentalists." I didn't answer since the timbre of her voice was the same as it would have been if she had said, "I'll bet you're a leper." She wasn't finished. "And I'll bet you're one of those bigots who say that Jesus is the only way to salvation."

I breathed a quick prayer. The last thing I wanted to do was get into a fight—verbal or otherwise—with Edith. It's not a great way to share the Good News. "Actually," I began. "I don't say this about the exclusive claims of Christ." She looked at me quizzically. "I don't need to," I continued, "because Jesus said this about Himself. He's the one Who said that He is the only way to God. I guess you'll need to take your concerns to Him."

Edith squeezed out a thin smile. She had already told me that she was an elder in a mainline church. She knew what I had said was true. And why was it true? Because it's in the Bible. Unequivocally.

Just like Jesus' testimony that "no one comes to the Father but by me," the admonition to wives about "submission" is in the Bible. There is no equivocation. Without sounding snarky, those who would prefer to argue with it will need to take it up with the Author.

In order to be obedient to God's Word, your wife must submit to your leadership. She is a lamb and you are her shepherd. Affirming this as truth could land this book in the recycling bin. I understand. I really do. Having spent almost thirty years as an elder in two churches aligned with "mainline" Protestant denominations, I'm picturing some of my friends at these churches. These folks may be looking up my email address in their contacts in order to send me a special message of condolence.

Many years ago, during a Sunday school class, I referred to a wife's duty of "submission"—the other "s" word in some people's minds. Afterwards, a friend approached me with concern. "I know men—husbands—whose wives have tried this submission route," he began. "They have done their best to honor and respect their husbands. They have willingly deferred leadership to him in their marriage."

"So far so good, I thought to myself, but I knew that my friend had more to say, so I continued to listen.

"But these guys are brutes. They take their wife's submission as license to be rude and thoughtless. They say that they love their wives but they roll their eyes in condescension when she speaks." I continued to listen carefully. "In my opinion," he said, apparently coming in for a landing, "I believe the feminist movement may have largely been born of Christian women who had had enough. They tried the submission thing, and all it got them was frustration and indignity."

I remember this moment as though it were last week. I thanked my friend for his candor, but my mind was spinning. In mentioning these verses, had I misled the married women in the class? Had I set them up for frustration in their marriages, maybe even abuse? Were the apostle's instructions obsolete? As I walked to my car, the words of the Australian activist Irina Dunn rang in my ears: "A woman needs a man like a fish needs a bicycle."

In the months that followed, I continued to think about these things. Now it's been years, and for the first time, I'm putting my thoughts in writing. Wishing that I could be chatting with you over a cup of coffee rather than communicating through the impersonal medium of a book, I want to say something that might just be a game changer for you—and for your wife.

"THE FEMINIST MOVEMENT WAS BORN OF CHRISTIAN WOMEN WHO HAD HAD ENOUGH. THEY TRIED THE SUBMISSION THING, AND ALL IT GOT THEM WAS FRUSTRATION AND INDIGNITY."

The word "faith" is often used to describe someone's religious leanings, as in, "He's a man of deep faith." But that raises the question, faith in *what*? I may have faith in something that is true or faith in a mirage. It makes a difference which. So it is with the word "submission." To whom—or to what—is your wife being asked to submit? Fortunately, Paul answers that question, painting a vivid picture of a man—a shepherd—who actually deserves to have his wife submit to him.

You're a Shepherd

Thankfully, right after telling wives to submit to their husbands, Paul speaks to you and me—husbands:

"Husbands, love your wives, as Christ loved the church and gave himself up for her, that he might sanctify her, having cleansed her by the washing of water with the word, so that he might present the church to himself in splendor, without spot or wrinkle or any such thing, that she might be holy and without blemish. In the same way husbands should love their wives as their own bodies. He who loves his wife loves himself." (Ephesians 5:25–28)

You have heard the expression "setting the bar high." Well, what we've just read takes this expression to a breathtaking level, doesn't it? Here's a fact that you can take to the bank. If you love your bride as Jesus loves His, the church, then her submission to your leadership will be a thrill for her.

Perhaps your chest swells at the thought of being a leader. Maybe you're thinking, "Now you're talking! It's about time I get the respect I deserve around here." Actually, the leadership I'm talking about isn't the kind of leadership you may be accustomed to seeing. This leadership is a different sort all together. Why? Because games of intimidation, power, control, and manipulation are utterly ineffective in marriage. A leader who demands that he be taken seriously simply on the basis of his position of leadership is a weak leader.

A LEADER WHO DEMANDS THAT HE BE TAKEN SERIOUSLY SIMPLY ON THE BASIS OF HIS POSITION OF LEADERSHIP IS A WEAK LEADER.

Your first exposure to a man assuming leadership in marriage was your own dad. If he was a great example, you're truly fortunate. All you have to do now is follow in his footsteps. You're not going to have to look elsewhere for a model. But if his example wasn't so great, that's okay. There are other examples. Like Jesus Christ.

Do nothing out of selfish ambition or vain conceit, but in humility consider others better than yourselves. Each of you should look not only to your own interests, but also to the interests of others. Your attitude should be the same as that of Christ Jesus. (Philippians 2:3–5)

Jesus was God. He had more power than any man who ever walked the earth, yet His life was a flawless example of the kind of leadership you need to take with your wife.

In His own words, here's Jesus' correct view of being "in charge."

You know that the rulers of the Gentiles lord it over them, and their high officials exercise authority over them. Not so with you. Instead, whoever wants to become great among you must be your servant, and whoever wants to be first must be your slave—just as the Son of Man did not come to be served, but to serve, and to give his life as a ransom for many. (Matthew 20:25–28)

Servanthood is the heart of leadership—effective shepherding—in your marriage. This is pleasing to God.

Husbands who demand that their wives submit to them have missed the point of godly leadership altogether. They are like the cartoon king who stomps around the castle shouting, "*I'm* in charge around here!" Men who act like this are only revealing their own insecurity. They're afraid that if they don't make angry demands, no one will follow them. "Not so with you," Jesus said. Not so with you. Not so with me.

So our journey has begun. In the remainder of this book, we will explore what a husband's Christ-like shepherding looks like. The goal is to give you specific ideas along with plenty of encouragement. My hope and prayer is that these chapters will be instructive and helpful.

FIVE

A SHEPHERD KNOWS HIS SHEEP

*Know well the condition of your flocks,
and give attention to your herds....*

—PROVERBS 27:23

How well do you know your wife?

Isn't it great when you know the answer to a question? Really know it? When teachers or professors asked questions in class and the answer was on the tip of your tongue, this was great fun. You shot your hand in the air, hoping you'd get picked. Years of watching the television quiz show *Jeopardy* reminded me of the delight of "knowing."

The first two times the verb "to know" appears in the Bible are in connection with marriage. The first instance of knowing comes immediately after Adam and Eve have eaten the forbidden fruit:

"Then the eyes of both were opened, and they *knew* that they were naked. And they sewed fig leaves together and made themselves loincloths." (Genesis 3:7, Italics added)

Adam and Eve were newlyweds. Everything in the Garden was perfect. Pristine. Their surroundings and their marriage were flawless. And then came the serpent, a question put to the woman, a passive husband, a bite of forbidden fruit—and perfect is gone. Scrubbed. Deleted. Bleached. In that moment, Adam and Eve saw their own bodies in a new way. They had been naked all along, but now they "knew" it. This knowing connotes absolute transparency. They were naked before; but now, because of their acquiescence to sin, their vulnerability was apparent.

You and your wife are sinners. My wife and I are, too. We have our first parents to thank for this. Like going outside on a cold day without a sweater, the sin of Adam and Eve gave rise to a new vulnerability, exposed them to the new reality of their true character—their sinful nature.

Making Love Takes Time

The second instance of "knowing" may surprise you.

Now Adam knew Eve his wife, and she conceived and bore Cain, saying, "I have gotten a man with the help of the LORD." (Genesis 4:1)

When you sleep with your wife, when you have sexual intercourse with her, you are "knowing" her. And doing this right can take a great deal of time. One of the peculiarities of lovemaking is that it generally takes far less time for you to be "ready" than your wife. Your climax can happen in a matter of minutes. Not so much with her.

By God's design, it takes time for your wife to be prepared to receive you. And this preparation is not only physiological—and, of course, it *is* that—but her readiness must be fully encircled. It's psychological, emotional, spiritual, physiological. Although you could press her into having sex with you any time, this will not turn out well for her. And, ultimately, not for you either. I'm picturing a shepherd, leading a sheep rather than a wrangler driving cattle. In order for your wife to get, as they say, "from here to there," you will need to be tender, gentle, and patient.

To help make this point more understandable, Barbara Brown Taylor tells what she learned from a friend who grew up on a sheep farm.

"[S]heep are not dumb at all. It is the cattle ranchers who are responsible for spreading that ugly rumor, and all because sheep do not behave like cows. According to my friend, cows are herded from the rear by hooting cowboys with cracking whips, but that will not work with sheep at all. Stand behind sheep making loud noises and all they will do is run around behind you, because they prefer to be led. You *push* cows, my friend said, but you *lead* sheep...."[1]

Satisfying lovemaking requires two things of you: patience and tenderness. This is why occasional get-aways with just the two of you are a great investment. No distractions. No interruptions. No kids standing outside your locked bedroom door, trying to get you to respond to them. Complete focus on each other, with time to spare. This is a good idea.

And if you're not sure about her satisfaction, ask her—but not "in the moment." At another time and place, tell your wife that you're eager that your lovemaking be a wonderful experience *for her*. Invite her to tell you what works and what doesn't. Then, when she tells you, listen carefully. Your goal is that your intimacy with her makes your wife feel secure, safe, loved.

You're Not Finished When You Think You're Finished

As I said, in lovemaking, you are likely to reach climax before— maybe long before—your wife does. And, physiologically, your body is telling you that you're finished. You wooed. You're satisfied. You're done.

Not so fast, tenderfoot. Even though your body has reached its euphoric pinnacle, your wife may still want—need—your tenderness, your touching, your caress.

Years ago my Chevy had a problem turning off. Even when the ignition key was turned to the left, the engine kept bumping and running—"dieseling," they call it. After you've been intimate with your wife, your ignition may be in the off position, but it's possible that your wife's engine is still running—dieseling. Hold her and touch her until she's completely settled. When I say that a shepherd *knows* his sheep, this tenderness and patience is what I mean.

EVEN THOUGH YOUR BODY HAS REACHED ITS EUPHORIC PINNACLE, YOUR WIFE MAY STILL WANT—NEED— YOUR TENDERNESS, YOUR TOUCHING, YOUR CARESS.

One more suggestion: Never, under any circumstances, tell anyone about any of this experience with your wife. Unless you're talking to a highly trained expert, keep all of this "in the vault."

The Tale of Three Gerunds

I'll bet you can't wait to read about this. Three gerunds? Sounds like fun, doesn't it? Recalling high school English class, you're probably saying to yourself, "I think I remember what a gerund is, but go ahead and remind me."

When you add "ing" to a verb, making it a noun, that's a gerund. "When I mix mortar, I realize that it's the most physically taxing part of bricklaying." Here "mix" is a verb. "Mixing mortar is the most physically taxing part of bricklaying." Here "mixing" is a noun. Got it? Well done.

So who cares about gerunds and what about the tale of three of them? I'm glad you asked.

UNLIKE FISHING AND HUNTING, OUR THIRD GERUND—"SHEPHERDING"—HAS A DESTINATION.

Early one morning not long after I had moved to Michigan, the sound of a rifle pierced the still, cold air. "What's that?" I asked Nancy.

"Gunshots," she responded, remembering that this was my first winter hunting season in Michigan. And then it dawned on me—the first gerund. "Hunting" is something lots of men do here in the north.

Consider the word "hunting." It speaks of dissatisfaction, of not quite getting there, as in, "Honey, do you know where my car keys are? I've been hunting all over the house for them." As long as you're hunting, you're not finding.

The second gerund is "fishing." Women who carry those huge purses know about this. Speaking of lost car keys, her purse is so large that it may take five minutes of fishing before she finds them. Like hunting, fishing suggests dissatisfaction. Now, how many men do you know who spend lots and lots (and lots) of time hunting and fishing? Maybe you're one of them. That's good.

Unlike fishing and hunting, our third gerund—"shepherding"—has a destination. Unlike hunting and fishing, this is a task you complete, a responsibility you fulfill. It's not a longing word. It's a word with a goal. Granted it's going to take time, but you and I can successfully shepherd. Several years ago, I ran into this verse tucked way back in the Old Testament. It proves that marriage—shepherding your wife—isn't a no-destination assignment.

If a man has recently married, he must not be sent to war or have any other duty laid on him. For one year he is to be free to stay at home and bring happiness to the wife he has married. (Deuteronomy 24:5)

JUST AS PATIENCE IS NECESSARY IN LOVEMAKING, THE WHOLE PROCESS OF KNOWING YOUR WIFE CANNOT BE HURRIED.

Can you imagine an ancient Israelite walking into his boss's office? "Uh, sir," he begins. "You know I'm getting married next month." His boss nods, but suspecting there's more to be said, sits quietly. Sure enough: "And I'd like to ask for some time off for my honeymoon."

The boss smiles, remembering the joy of his own honeymoon many years before. "How much time off would you like?"

"A year!" the brave young man says.

We smile at this scenario. How silly. A whole year for a honeymoon? But there's a great deal of wisdom here. Just as patience is necessary in lovemaking, the whole process of knowing your wife cannot be hurried. I admit that a year seems a bit unreasonable these days, but if you're going to be a knowledgeable shepherd, learning the sweet nuances and idiosyncrasies of your sheep takes time.

Practice Times Three

With 1,210 wins and 694 career losses, Pat Riley is one of professional basketball's most successful coaches. His mini-camps are legendary. When asked why he and his teams have been so successful, Riley gives his trademark response: "Practice. Practice. Practice."

Getting it right in your marriage requires practice. That's for sure. However—and this might surprise you—shepherding your marriage is not only about practice; it's also about winning. It's about being the first to make adjustments in order to demonstrate love for your wife. It means being the first to serve, the first to forgive, and the first to sacrifice your convenience. Winning. This describes the radical and sacrificial love of Jesus the Good Shepherd.

Fifty-One Percent Ownership

In 1986, when Michael Hyatt and I founded Wolgemuth & Hyatt Publishers, we decided, on the advice of our attorney, to divide the ownership of the company 51-49 percent and not 50-50. Because I was a little older with a few more years of publishing experience under my belt, Mike suggested I should take the larger share of ownership. I agreed. But at that moment—and I'll never forget it—I quietly resolved never to use my majority stake to force anything on my business partner. My job was to handle some of the more cumbersome tasks of the business and to help him to develop his skills and gifts. And I never told him about this decision. My success was going to show up as his success.

It's true that you and your wife are each 100 percent "stakeholders" in your marriage. But as the shepherd, borrowing the example from my own business experience, you and I are the 51 percent "owners" in our marriage. And if your wife knew that this role would inspire you to heroic service, she would choose it for you herself. It's the shepherd she's looking for. You're it.

Fighting for Her

When I was a little boy, my parents had a strict "no guns" policy. You never saw my brothers or me with toy guns hanging from our belts. But what my dad and mother didn't realize was that we could make do with a banana, a stick, a pencil, a telephone, a piece of uncooked spaghetti, a sleeping cat, a young sibling, a finger, a stuffed animal...you get the idea.

Aggression is hardwired into every man. We love to conquer. As George Will explains, "During the seventh or eighth week in the womb, boy babies are infused with an explosive male hormone called testosterone. It makes little boys aggressive. In all societies, men are more likely than women to play roughly, drive recklessly, and fight."[2] Most boys were made to duke it out.

As husbands—shepherds—our job is to win the chance to gently lead, to fight for the chance to woo our sheep with humility and kindness. We can spend our lives climbing the corporate ladder, battling opponents in the courtroom, winning tennis tournaments, or combating disease in the operating room. But men who don't give their best effort in their role as shepherd more often than not find themselves fighting the wrong battles. If the sheep are left without a shepherd, winning doesn't really matter.

AGGRESSION IS HARDWIRED INTO EVERY MAN. WE LOVE TO CONQUER.

In 2005, 1,500 sheep ran off a cliff in a remote village in Turkey. Only 450 perished, their bodies cushioning the fall for the 1,050 who followed. The news reports gave no explanation for the mass suicide, but it seems that the shepherds had slipped away for breakfast. One sheep jumped and, apparently, the others followed. As we saw with Shrek the Unshorn, sheep tend to get in serious trouble if they have no shepherd.

Unwilling Sheep?

At this point, there may be a question brewing in your mind. "Okay," you may be saying. "So I'm going to embrace my role as my wife's shepherd. I'm not going to take my Deuteronomic year off from work, I'm not even going to take an irresponsibly long breakfast break, but I am going to become an expert on my wife and get serious about being her shepherd. But what if my wife has no interest in being led? What if she defies my attempts to shepherd her? What then?"

That's an important question, and there's really only one good answer. You have no power to change your wife. However long you've been married, you have probably tried and come up short. Why? Because only God can change your wife's heart, and He will do so when she decides to listen to His voice. And so you lovingly pray for her to understand. And your prayer is that you will become the kind of shepherd that she willingly follows. You can decide to be a good shepherd. Following will need to be her decision.

A True Story

I have told you something of the strength, talent, and wisdom of the two women whom I have had the privilege of calling my wife. What interest would such remarkable women have in being led by their husband? Their willingness to view me as the head of our marriage and to let me lead flowed not from a sense of inadequacy or need but from their conviction of spiritual calling.

God did a work in their hearts and they obeyed His voice.

Rosaria Butterfield, a dear friend of ours, grew up in a home of "committed unbelievers" and became a professor of English at a major state university, publishing and teaching in the fields of nineteenth-century literature and feminist theory. She was also the LGBTQ faculty sponsor at her campus. Rosaria was fiercely independent and openly hostile to the Gospel and to Christians who embrace biblical truth. Eventually, however, through the humble witness of a pastor and his wife who reached out in love and hospitality to her and her lesbian partner, Rosaria's eyes were opened and, by faith, she received Jesus as her Savior. In time, she married Kent Butterfield, a pastor, and they lovingly adopted four transracial children, two of whom were adopted out of foster care at the age of seventeen.

> WHAT IF MY WIFE HAS NO INTEREST IN BEING LED? WHAT IF SHE DEFIES MY ATTEMPTS TO SHEPHERD HER? WHAT THEN?

In a conversation with my wife, Nancy, on her *Revive Our Hearts* radio program, Rosaria talked about her role in her marriage, and the role of the shepherd is clear:

"The Lord has molded Kent and me into a one-flesh-ness that really has developed and has grown and matured out of our spiritual connection. Husbands have a powerfully difficult role as heads of households…they are dying to themselves. I have been really blessed by learning to submit to Kent's spiritual headship and by learning to rest in his authority. That's been really crucial.

"I got married at thirty-nine years old.… I had been a professional woman my whole life, and now I'm committed to being a submitted wife, because I know that that gives glory to God and respect to my husband. I'm really grateful that the Lord knew I needed Kent Butterfield to be my husband and to be my head.

"I'm so glad that I already—by God's grace—worked through an understanding that Kent's headship over me was God's protection over me. So, when we have had hard decisions, often Kent and I tend to share a similar way of approaching things, but Kent makes the ultimate and final call on things. I can rest in that, even if at the time I might see things differently. And I can appeal to my Lord as I'm praying for Kent."

When I heard Rosaria say these things to Nancy, I was both stunned and encouraged. Here's a woman who was once an ardent feminist but now finds great joy in following the biblical pattern for marriage.

The Lost Art of Being Lost

Of all the technologies that take my breath away, the global positioning system (GPS) is at the top. The voice coming from my phone or dashboard telling me exactly where I am and how to get where I want to go was unimaginable just a few years ago. But with the advent of GPS, paper maps have gone the way of the buggy whip.

Growing up, I was a map guy—a paper map guy. I think I gained appreciation for them when I first saw them spread out on my mother's lap as she rode shotgun on family car trips. When I bought my first car as a junior in college, I filled the glove compartment with a stash of neatly folded maps. Seeing the big picture—where I was and where I was headed—gave me a feeling of security and, when I arrived at my destination, accomplishment. I hated getting lost. Even writing the word "lost" gives me a sinking feeling in my stomach.

And then came GPS. Although I miss the big picture that a paper map provides, I appreciate having "someone" talk me from point A to point B. No muss. No fuss. No getting lost.

Always knowing where we are and where we're going and exactly what time we're going to arrive, we have forgotten the awful sensation of being lost. So when we talk about the wonder of having a shepherd lead us or find us, it's easy to overlook the emotional trauma of getting lost. Being lost can be terrifying.

The Lost Sheep

In the fifteenth chapter of the Gospel of Luke, Jesus tells stories about three lost things—a sheep, a coin, and a son. The third story fills most of the chapter, so it tends to overshadow the other two. In fact, the whole chapter is often referred to as the story of the Prodigal Son.

But we shouldn't overlook the first story:

So [Jesus] told them this parable: "What man of you, having a hundred sheep, if he has lost one of them, does not leave the ninety-nine in the open country, and go after the one that is lost, until he finds it? And when he has found it, he lays it on his shoulders, rejoicing. And when he comes home, he calls together his friends and his neighbors, saying to them, 'Rejoice with me, for I have found my sheep that was lost.'" (Luke 15:3–6)

This story is a parable. Jesus made it up to make a point. And what was His point? Here's my take. Luke tells us that Jesus' audience consisted of two groups—"tax collectors and sinners" and "the Pharisees and the scribes" (15:2). The former were considered riffraff by the elites. Tax collectors were traitors, raising money from their own people for the occupying Romans. "Sinners" were those not clever enough to avoid getting caught doing what almost everyone else did. I picture Jesus teaching these people in a casual setting, perhaps outdoors. And because the "tax collectors and sinners" understood their low social standing, they were the hungriest and most vulnerable, likely sitting close to the Teacher.

Earlier, Jesus had dined with the notorious tax collector Matthew, indicating the kind of people He had come to save:

> **THIS SHEPHERD IS SERIOUS, FOCUSED, INTENTIONAL. HE NOT ONLY KNOWS HIS MATH, HE KNOWS HIS SHEEP.**

And the scribes of the Pharisees, when they saw that he was eating with sinners and tax collectors, said to his disciples, "Why does he eat with tax collectors and sinners?" And when Jesus heard it, he said to them, "Those who are well have no need of a physician, but those who are sick. I came not to call the righteous, but sinners." (Mark 2:16–17)

As I imagine the scene where the story of the lost things was being told, Christ's listeners are sitting in concentric semicircles, the worst of them—sinners—in the front, "drawing near to Jesus." Farther out sit the Pharisees and the scribes. As Jesus begins his stories, He looks into the eyes of the men sitting at His feet. And even though He has already called both groups of listeners "sheep without a shepherd" (Matthew 9:36), the focus of at least the first story is on the closer ones, those most apparently lost and in need of a shepherd.

In those days, a hundred sheep were a moderately sized flock, and tending them would have been a full-time job. Jesus doesn't give us many details—just that a man had a hundred sheep and one of them got lost. Jesus also hints that the other ninety-nine were confined, protected somehow, perhaps in a sheepfold. The shepherd didn't leave these sheep in "open country" when he left to search for the lost one.

We could take away a number of lessons from this story—sheep's proclivity to wander, or the shepherd's willingness to leave everything to find the lost one. But my favorite lesson from the story is simply this—the shepherd knows his sheep. This is not a passive herdsman, not the "hireling" who "sees the wolf coming and leaves the sheep and flees" (John 10:12). This shepherd is serious, focused, intentional. He not only knows his math, he knows his sheep.

Your Wife

By recalling this parable of the lost sheep, I'm not suggesting that your wife is a wanderer, that someday you'll come home and find her gone. Although I do know men to whom that has happened, it's not what I'm talking about. But please pay attention to the following.

Can you remember reciting your wedding vows to your bride? The actual moment when you looked into her eyes and promised "to love and to cherish, till death us do part"? I did this in March 1970 and again in November 2015. And in each case I remember with absolute clarity the resolution and certainty of the woman standing before me, serious and sober about what she was telling me. And her eyes were telling me that her heart was home. She was safe.

AND HER EYES WERE TELLING ME THAT HER HEART WAS HOME. SHE WAS SAFE.

Maybe you had the same feeling. But in the weeks and months following that exchange of vows, there came a moment that you realized that your hearts were further apart than they had been at the altar. Because my marriage to Nancy is the more recent, I vividly remember this look from her.

Less than a month after our wedding in Chicago, we settled for a few weeks of Christmas celebration in a small home in the Carolinas. This was close to my children and grandchildren, and Nancy and I were looking forward to spending time with them. A few days after our arrival, the washing machine turned the first floor of the house into a wading pool. The next three weeks saw a parade of contractors and, thankfully, an insurance adjuster who agreed to cover the costs. But the weeks Nancy and I had intended to hang out with our kids and grandkids and each other—and also get some work done—were spent in a small upstairs bedroom. With just enough room for two overstuffed chairs facing each other and an ottoman in between, we spent almost three weeks doing our work facing each other.

In the ten months since we had begun dating, we had spent many hours together. The majority of this time was spent sitting on a couch facing a fireplace or in a restaurant across the corner of a square table. But not literally face to face. At least not three weeks of every waking hour, face to face.

One afternoon in our small, cramped headquarters, the conversation turned to a difficult situation related to my business. Seeing things from different perspectives, we fleshed out our thoughts and strong opinions. As we talked, we both expressed emotion regarding our view of what had happened. The more we talked, the more I felt a growing distance between our hearts. It would have been easy to disregard the uncertainty I felt at that moment. After all, I had a lot of work to do, including writing this book. Surely we would get over what we were feeling at that moment and soon life would return to normal. Maybe. But I pushed through my apprehensions and tried to put words to what I was perceiving, thinking, and feeling.

In retrospect, this conversation was our first "hard talk." The euphoria of our wedding and honeymoon were behind us and life as it was going to be was taking root. And the best way I can describe my experience in this moment is that our hearts seemed to be in a different place than they had been a few minutes before.

And so we talked. Was Nancy grateful for the chance to verbally unpack her feelings in that moment? A safe place to speak with candor? Yes, absolutely.

But the door to our hearts needed to be opened. We were both focused on our work. We appeared to be sitting in the same room, concentrating on what needed to be done. Our bodies were in that little upstairs alcove, but our minds were not there at all.

Years ago, I heard the great, Jesus-following motivational speaker Zig Ziglar in person. He said something that made his audience laugh, but when I heard him say it, I didn't laugh. And I haven't forgotten what he said. Zig told us that even though we looked like we were sitting there listening to him, many of us were "somewhere else." He told us that a few of us were working on tomorrow's meeting schedules; some were having a silent conversation with a person with whom they were in a difficult relationship. "Some of you," Zig said with that Mississippi twang, "are at home cookin' dinner. You look like you're here, but you're not here." Everyone laughed. But, of course, he was right. We were still physically in his presence, but our minds had wandered off.

This perfectly describes what was going on between Nancy and me.

Racing to the Cross

When she was young, my daughter Julie loved to get lost. This was actually a game. It happened in department stores, where there

YOU ARE YOUR WIFE'S SHEPHERD. YOU HAVE THE JOY OF CARING FOR HER, BUT YOU WILL OCCASIONALLY FAIL.

were lots of good places to hide. I remember concern escalating to worry and then to sheer panic. "Where's Julie?" I'd ask out loud. But since this was just a game (to Julie), her happy face would eventually pop out from behind a counter or from between clothes hanging on a rack. Scooping up her little frame, I'd feel relieved and then angry that she had put me through this drama one more time.

Just like the conscientious shepherd in Jesus' parable, you have the commission to seek after your wife when you suspect that her heart might be distracted or headed somewhere mysterious.

I've really never thought about this before, but can you imagine the shepherd's retrieving his wandering lamb after the search and then feeling the same mix of relief and anger that I felt when I found Julie in the department store? We can even imagine a "conversation" between the shepherd and the lamb:

Shepherd: I was so worried. How good it is to find you and to hold you.

Sheep: I'm sorry that I wandered off. I didn't mean to frighten you. Thank you for loving me so much that you'd strike out in the darkness to search for me.

Shepherd: Of course. You're my sheep. I should have been more careful. I was distracted and not paying attention to you. Please forgive me.

Sheep: I forgive you. And thank you for forgiving me.

This conversation between shepherd and sheep might be silly speculation, but you get the idea. This is you and your wife. We call such a conversation "racing to the cross." The goal is to see who can be the first one to get to the cross of Jesus for forgiveness and reconciliation.

You are your wife's shepherd. You have the joy of caring for her, but you will often fail. You are responsible for protecting her, but you will occasionally be distracted. You are committed to loving her, but there will be times when she won't feel loved. And so you'll admit your failure in spite of good intentions. You'll receive forgiveness and move on.

Your wife will appreciate this. I promise.

SIX

A SHEPHERD SPEAKS TO HIS SHEEP

My sheep hear my voice, and I know them,
and they follow me.

—JOHN 10:27

I magine that we are standing in front of a large gathering of Christian men. I mean a *large* gathering—thousands of guys. And let's say that these men have a robust working knowledge of the Bible. They're active in a church and are part of a small group of friends who study the Scriptures together. Then I say to the audience, "What I'm about to tell you is one of the most dramatic stories in the Bible." And I ask everyone to tell me in a text message which story he thinks I'm talking about. The results are tallied and projected on the big screen, with lots of votes for Abraham's sacrifice of Isaac, the parting of the Red Sea, David and Goliath, and the death of Samson. It's a safe bet that not one of those men would vote for the story I'm about to tell them.

No Plan

Sibling rivalry was a chronic problem among the Hebrew Patriarchs. Having cheated his older brother, Esau, out of his birthright, Jacob poisoned relations among his own twelve sons by officially designating the eleventh, Joseph, as his favorite. The young man didn't help matters by tactlessly recounting to his older brothers his visions of their bowing before him in homage, and soon enough the older boys were plotting to kill him. The fortuitous appearance of a caravan bound for Egypt, however, presented the opportunity of selling Joseph into slavery, a more profitable way of disposing of the irksome lad than fratricide and easier on the conscience. But God had other plans for Joseph, as everyone would eventually discover.

Twenty years later, because of a drought, the once bountiful land of Canaan, where Jacob and his sons lived, had become a useless desert, its inhabitants afflicted with famine. Egypt, on the other hand, having providently stockpiled its grain according to Joseph's directions, was riding out the lean years unperturbed. "When Jacob learned that there was grain for sale in Egypt, he impatiently said to his sons, 'Why do you look at one another?'" (Genesis 42:1) The old man sent his dithering sons—all but the youngest, Benjamin, "for he feared that harm might befall him"—into Egypt to buy grain.

IN AN ACT OF MERCY AND FORGIVENESS, JOSEPH DRAWS HIS BROTHERS TOGETHER. HE GATHERS THEM IN HIS ARMS, AND THEY TALK.

The weeks that followed were filled with the kind of drama that a Hollywood producer would drool over. The sons of Jacob came before the governor seeking to buy grain, but because of his Egyptian language and costume they did not recognize their brother Joseph. He recognized them, however. Longing to see his younger brother but keeping his identity a secret, Joseph devised a pretext to induce them to bring Benjamin to Egypt. When they eventually presented the boy to him, Joseph, overcome with emotion, cleared the room of his attendants and disclosed his identity to his astonished brothers. Can you imagine the look on their chalky faces when the governor of Egypt, who held their lives in his hands, declared simply, "I am Joseph; is my father still alive?"[1]

The scene that followed is what makes me call this one of the most dramatic stories in the Bible. Joseph revealed to them all that had happened since they had sold him into slavery, explaining how God in His providence had used their murderous scheme "to preserve for [them] a remnant on earth, and to keep alive for [them] many survivors" (Genesis 45:7). "Then he fell upon his brother Benjamin's neck and wept, and Benjamin wept upon his neck. And he kissed all his brothers and wept upon them; and after that his brothers talked with him." (45:14–15)

In an act of mercy and forgiveness, Joseph draws his brothers together. He gathers them in his arms, and they talk. I can imagine the tears of remorse as the older brothers confessed their treachery in trying to do away with their bratty little brother. In their conversation, there surely were stories of the homeland and the twists and turns of living in a growing and extensive family.

The Magic Bridge

I wrote my first book in 1996. The idea came to me on a long car trip with Mike Hyatt, and his wife, Gail. The Hyatts had five daughters; Bobbie and I had two. So with seven girls between us, Mike and I discussed the big responsibility we had in being "Daddy" to them. A few months later I started work on what became the book *She Calls Me Daddy*.

Reviewing what I had learned—some of it the hard way—about being a father to daughters, I identified some important principles, a sturdy bridge to get us safely from one side of the sometimes raging river to the other. One of them is conversation:

Properly teaching the skills of conversation is the most critical thing a dad must do in building his little girl. The ability for you and your daughter to effectively exchange words—and the feelings they're usually connected to—will provide the bridge between you that will last the rest of your lives.[2]

The conversation bridge between you and your wife is no less essential than that between a dad and his daughter. In fact, it's more important. Getting conversation right between you and your wife will be great training for you and your daughter (or son)—and someday your granddaughter (or grandson).

Go back in your memory to the time when you and your wife were dating. Maybe you sat and talked by the hour. Nothing else, just talking. And there was so much to talk about. In these conversations you learned about each other's story and family. You discovered what was important to each other. You celebrated common convictions and mutual interests.

The image of the bridge really works here, doesn't it? And depending on the differences between your backgrounds and families of origin, it may be a simple wooden arch over a garden stream or something more like the Golden Gate.

Over the years, when I have taught classes on the art of conversation and effective communication, I've written three numbers on the white board—55, 38, and 7—and asked my students what they think they represent. The answer: when you're talking with your wife, 55 percent of what is actually communicated is the look on your face or other body language, 38 percent is your tone of voice, and only 7 percent is the words you speak.[3]

If this is true, why even bother talking about talking? Because actually putting things into words is the most effective way to express love, confess a breach, or clarify intentions. In fact, body language and voice inflection are usually connected to spoken words, so paying special attention to verbal communication is not a waste of time. Talking about talking is important.

Either way, saying the right things to your wife is not a negotiable.

Tenderness Wins

Like the sun in Aesop's fable, your tender words warm your wife's spirit. And they win your wife's heart.

Yes, I know that life does not consist primarily of nonstop cuddling and whispering sweet nothings. There are schedules to coordinate, children to discipline, trash to take out, meals to prepare, broken water pipes to fix (and floors to mop up). As the bumper sticker boldly announces, "Life Happens" (or something like that).

But when you take the time to speak tenderly to your wife, she will feel secure and safe with you. And she may even respond to you with the same kind of tenderness. When she does, you will experience the kind of joy she does when you're tender with her.

The power of tenderness is beautifully illustrated in one of my favorite movies, *Sommersby*, a 1993 retelling of the case of the sixteenth-century French impostor Martin Guerre, set in the American South during Reconstruction. Six years after Jack Sommersby left his wife, Laurel, and farm to fight in the Civil War, a man purporting to be Sommersby returns. While Sommersby had been a hard and abusive husband before his departure, now he is kind and generous. It transpires that this man is really Horace Townsend, who shared a prison cell with the real Sommersby, learning enough about the life of his cellmate, now dead, to fool his neighbors.

> BUT WHEN YOU TAKE THE TIME TO SPEAK TENDERLY TO YOUR WIFE, SHE WILL FEEL SECURE AND SAFE WITH YOU.

We learn, however, that he did not fool Laurel, who nevertheless accepted Townsend as her husband. When his imposture eventually forces him to stand trial for murder as Jack Sommersby, Laurel, to save his life, admits that she has known all along that he is not her husband. Pressed by Townsend on how she knew that he was not the abusive man she had known, Laurel in tears replies, "Because I never loved him the way I love you!"

It's clear that the real Sommersby had been harsh with his wife. Sacrificing sweet intimacy, he had opted for the drive for success. Townsend, on the other hand, had won her with tenderness. Making demands and rough talk will not win the day with our wives. We are not wranglers. We are shepherds. Good shepherds.

I Will Go First

Even the most untroubled couples face a challenge when it comes to spoken communication. When there's a breach of any kind in your marriage, when ice is forming around the edges and someone needs to break it, who goes first? Who steps out and risks?

Let me suggest that the risk-taker could be you. Just as the biggest step in your day may be putting your bare feet down on the cold floor next to your bed, the biggest obstacle to healing communication with your wife can be uttering those first words— "Honey, let's take some time to talk about this."

> MAKING DEMANDS AND ROUGH TALK WILL NOT WIN THE DAY WITH OUR WIVES. WE ARE NOT COWBOYS. WE ARE SHEPHERDS. GOOD SHEPHERDS.

Look back over the times in your life when you've needed to talk something over with a friend or a colleague—or an enemy, for that matter. How often were you glad that you took the initiative? Fifty percent of the time? More? In my experience, it's a lot

more. In fact, the answer is nearly 100 percent of the time.

And let me add a suggestion that may
sound obvious as you sit here reading a book.
Treat your wife like your friend. Ask yourself,
"How would I speak to a friend about this?"

The Bible calls going back to the way it
was when you were dating, when you were
wooing your sweetheart, "returning to your
first love" (Revelation 2:4). A good shepherd
speaks to his sheep—tender words reminis-
cent of the words he spoke when he and she
first met and his objective was to win her.

You can do this again.

> **UNLIKE MONEY IN YOUR
> SAVINGS ACCOUNT AND
> FINE WINE, UNSPOKEN
> WORDS THAT NEED TO
> BE EXPRESSED USUALLY
> DO NOT AGE WELL.
> THEY DO NOT FERMENT
> TO PERFECTION.
> MORE OFTEN THAN
> NOT, THEY SPOIL.**

Compound Interest

Unlike money in your savings account and fine wine, unspoken
words that need to be expressed usually do not age well. They do not
ferment to perfection. More often than not, they spoil.

If you're like most couples, you and your wife have different
approaches to keeping "relationship accounts." One of you seems
content to let disagreements brew and stew; the other drives to conflict resolution like a fullback getting close to the end zone. But
whatever your approach, let me suggest, based on experience, that
going to bed with unresolved conflict is never a good idea. By morning, you'll both have largely forgotten the problem. After a few hours
of sleep, the urgency and the important details of the fracture are
forgotten—for the time being.

Unattended trouble grows like compound interest. Small problems become medium-size problems, and medium-size problems

become big problems. Soon you've got serious trouble. What's needed is air. Release. And that begins with words. Words like, "I'm sorry. I was wrong. Will you please forgive me?"

The Power of Words

"Look at the ships also: though they are so large and are driven by strong winds, they are guided by a very small rudder wherever the will of the pilot directs. So also the tongue is a small member, yet it boasts of great things." (James 3:4–5)

The Apostle James's observation about the power of the rudder over the ships crisscrossing the Mediterranean in the first century is all the more impressive when applied to the giant oceangoing vessels of the modern world. A timely turn of the rudder of the *Titanic* that April night in 1912 would have saved 1,500 lives. This, according to God's Word, is the power that our words wield.

We say that the First Amendment guarantees our right to "free speech," but there is often a heavy price to pay or a priceless reward to claim for the words we speak: "Will you marry me?" "Guilty, Your Honor." "I'm leaving you." "I love you." Words are powerful and precious, and you and your wife are connected by them.

Ancient Wisdom about Words

Few figures in the Old Testament had King Solomon's way with words. Such was his appreciation of their power that he wrote, "A word fitly spoken is like apples of gold in a setting of silver." (Proverbs 25:15)

The bridge of words we're building with our wives is priceless. Our goal is that each word we use be weighted down with plenty of wisdom and humility and care. Words "fitly spoken."

SEVEN

A Shepherd Satisfies His Sheep

I can't get no satisfaction.

—Mick Jagger, 1965

Many years ago, a friend—I'll call him Kyle—and I had just enjoyed lunch together. I had known him for many years, and our conversation was free and easy. As we drove back to his house, we spotted a brown delivery truck parked on his street, and the driver was walking up Kyle's driveway, a stack of packages in his arms. I will never forget the sound Kyle made at this sight—a strange blend of a groan and an angry hiss. "What's wrong?" I asked as I parked the car.

"I hate UPS," he replied.

Amazed that a delivery service could provoke such strong feelings, I pressed, "What's up with that?" For the next few minutes, Kyle poured out his heart, giving voice to a pain that came from somewhere

"IS IT POSSIBLE," I BEGAN, "THAT YOUR WIFE ISN'T SATISFIED BECAUSE SHE SEES AN UNFULFILLED SENSE OF LONGING IN YOU?"

deep inside. The problem, he said, was his wife's "out-of-control spending."

"It used to be that she'd go on shopping jags. And at least I'd have an idea that she was buying stuff. But now, with the ease of Internet, she spends money like we have it. She's out of control," he repeated. I turned slightly toward Kyle so I could see his face, but I did not say anything. "The real problem is that I'm afraid to question her," he confessed, deep emotion sweeping across his countenance. "I've tried to confront her about the spending, but her anger scares me. It's a minefield. If I keep going, my leg will get blown off. Or worse."

For a minute or two there was silence. I searched for something to say that would be helpful. Then the first line of the twenty-third Psalm, in the Living Bible's paraphrase, popped into my head: "Because the Lord is my Shepherd, I have everything that I need." Suddenly the answer to Kyle's dilemma appeared. But before I opened my mouth to offer my friend any advice, I realized that the counsel I was getting ready to offer was for me too.

"Is it possible," I began, "that your wife isn't satisfied because she sees an unfulfilled sense of longing in you?" And because I sensed that the Lord was not going to let me preach a sermon I wasn't living, I added, "I wonder if my wife sees the same lack of contentment in me."

Where Our Unfulfilled Longings Might Take Us

Jesus' parable of the lost sheep is not a story of open defiance. Unlike the Prodigal Son, that sheep did not shake his little hoof in the shepherd's hairy face and demand its freedom before taking off. No, he just got bored nibbling on the same tuft of grass. The same-ol' same-ol'. Then he looked up and saw what looked like a tastier tuft— just over there, not *that* far away. So he nibbled on this new tuft until the boredom crept in again. By the time darkness fell, the little guy was lost.

What started as a conversation between Kyle and me about the UPS truck turned into an exchange of confessions about how our wives were following our lead of disquiet and dissatisfaction. We admitted how the restless, entrepreneurial spirit that had led us both to start our own companies had infiltrated our hearts. Good for business. Bad for our souls. And bad for our marriages.

And how was this showing up? To start with, probably in our words.

I drive a nice car. Driving a nice car was important to my dad, so maybe I inherited the preoccupation from him. But because the urge to compare and compete is embedded in every Y chromosome, I can always spot a nicer car than mine on the road. Even watching a movie with my wife will bring this out. The other night in front of our big screen, I heard myself saying, "That's a Ferrari. It's a convertible and it's red." My wife did not respond. She knows that I notice, and that's okay. No response is necessary.

The other day, I met Greg, the guy who owns the gym where Nancy works out. Since Greg does this for a living, he's in better shape than I am—much better shape. I couldn't help but notice and mentioned it to my wife.

So is it possible that my wife is listening to my words and thinking, "Since Robert clearly doesn't have everything he needs, it seems obvious that he's not aware that the Lord is his Shepherd. If my husband is unsatisfied with his car or his body, then it must be okay for me to be that way as well."

See how this works?

Although I try to be a happy man, taking life's challenges and victories in stride, truth be known, I'm pretty restless and dissatisfied. I want to live like I have everything that I need, but deep inside there are unfulfilled longings that keep me unsatisfied. Tired of nibbling on the same tuft of grass, I often scan the surrounding pasture, looking for greener tufts.

You Don't Need to Own to Enjoy

If you'll let me, I'd love to step up on my little soapbox. This will just take a few minutes, I promise. But maybe it'll be helpful.

If you don't have a friend like Tony Allen, you should. Tony lives in Orlando. For many years, he and I were part of a special group of men called "DreamBuilders."[1] Every year, Tony hosts an exotic car festival in Celebration, Florida. A few years ago, I took my son-in-law (an even bigger car nut than I am) and his two teenage sons to this amazing display of steel, glass, chrome, power, and sheer four-wheeled beauty.

Our day was filled with oo's and ah's. We saw a production car that retails for more than a million dollars and the actual DeLorean from *Back to the Future*. We saw antique cars and freshly-minted models. My favorite was a Bentley Continental GT convertible. I even asked the owner, who was standing guard, if I could sit in it. He said yes, and I gently opened the door and settled in behind the wheel. Feeling the leather and scanning the dash, I inhaled. Oh my. What a day!

That night, before I went to sleep, I reviewed the experience. I lay there smiling, happily recalling the fun of being with my family on a beautiful spring day and taking in the beauty of those cars...the gleam, the colors, the smells. I drifted off to sleep feeling a great sense of satisfaction.

Does that surprise you? A car buff dropped in the middle of hundreds of the most magnificent vehicles ever made might feel thrilled or dazzled, but *satisfied*? Yes! Right before my son-in-law, my grandsons, and I entered the show, we all agreed that we didn't need to *own* any of those exotic cars to *enjoy* them. And so we did.

For a shepherd to satisfy the needs of his wife, his own heart must be satisfied. And the secret to achieving that satisfaction is this: "Because the Lord is my shepherd, I have everything that I need." Once we've embraced the love of our Good Shepherd for us and received the call to be His very own sheep, there is nothing—not even a Bentley Continental GT—that we don't have that we truly need. You and I have everything that we need. We can be satisfied.

He Left It All

Zig Ziglar used to tell the story about H. L. Hunt, the Texas oil tycoon who was one of the world's few billionaires when he died in 1974. "People have wondered how much wealth ol' Daddy Hunt left when he died," Zig used to twang. "I'll tell you how much he left." And flashing that amazing Yazoo City smile, he continued, "I'll tell you *exactly, precisely* how much ol' Daddy Hunt left behind. *He left it all.*"

In May 1988, at the age of ninety-nine, my maternal grandfather, Monroe Sharpe Dourte, died, survived by eight children, thirty-five grandchildren, and a full contingent of great- and great-great-grandchildren. One of his four sons, all ordained or licensed ministers, described Grandpa Dourte's "Last Will and Testament" at his funeral: "I, Monroe Dourte, leave all my wealth to my family. And there's no need to divide any of it. I give it to each of you in full."

WHAT YOUR WIFE NEEDS IS A HUSBAND WHO KNOWS THAT HE IS A SHEEP AND HE HAS A GOOD SHEPHERD.

None of us who were there had ever heard such a thing. We listened carefully. "I leave you my love for Jesus and His love for me. He is a Good Shepherd and He has given me everything I have ever wanted. All I have ever needed. And you, my family, can have this. All of it. In full. The dividing of my estate will not be necessary."

Monroe Dourte knew what it was to live with little. When my mother was a child, she and each of her seven siblings would receive a small bag of hard candy for Christmas. If it had been an especially good year at the farm, there might also be a Florida orange in the bag. But because he had laid up for himself "treasures in heaven," Monroe died a forgiven man. A satisfied man. A whole man. A faithful shepherd. He died an extremely wealthy man.

Stuff

Do you experience a strange gnawing in your stomach when Christmas, your wife's birthday, or your wedding anniversary approaches? I do, too. Whether you've been married for decades or are a newlywed, you know this feeling. If you'll let me, I'd love to tell you exactly what your wife is looking for the next time one of these special days arrives. It's not stuff, it cannot be bought online, and UPS can't deliver it with a brown truck.

What your wife needs is a husband who knows that he is a sheep and he has a Good Shepherd. She wants a man who has everything he needs, a man who may be driven and entrepreneurial and visionary when it comes to business but whose heart listens to the voice of Jesus, a satisfied man who obediently follows the Lord. She longs for a husband who submits to his tender heavenly Shepherd. This is what your wife wants; she longs to have this same kind of earthly shepherd.

She May Have This Problem
Worse than You Do

Whatever temptations to dissatisfaction you experience, your wife may have it worse. Do I have any evidence for that assertion? Yes, I do. Generalizations about "all women" or even "most women" can be extremely dangerous, of course, but here goes.

In Genesis chapter 3, we have an amazing account—a true story—of history's first wife. You remember that God had told Adam that he could have the run of the Garden of Eden. There was nothing there that was not his to enjoy—nothing, that is, but the fruit of a certain tree. God's instructions to Adam were precise:

The Lord God took the man and put him in the Garden of Eden to work it and keep it. And the Lord God commanded the man, saying, "You may surely eat of every tree of the garden, but of the tree of the knowledge of good and evil you shall not eat, for in the day that you eat of it you shall surely die." (Genesis 2:15–17)

Adam did not ask for an explanation or a second opinion. He had received specific instructions—and a warning—from his Creator. That should have been enough.

The next paragraph tells how God created Adam's wife (2:18–25). The third chapter introduces the serpent, "more subtle than any other wild creature that the LORD God had made," and continues with this remarkable twist: "[The serpent] said to the woman, 'Did God actually say, "You shall not eat of any tree in the garden?"'" (3:1).

It is clear from what follows (a) that Eve knew that God had forbidden her husband and her from eating the fruit of the tree of the knowledge of good and evil and (b) that Adam, who was passively standing right there,[2] didn't interrupt this dangerous conversation between his wife and the serpent. What are we to make of the way the exchange unfolded? How could things have turned out differently?

Tell Your Wife about Your Temptations

During the summers of my college education, I had the unique joy of working for a building contractor. Richard Whitmer was the father of one of my closest friends, and I was his only fulltime employee. To say that this man was skilled in every trade would only begin to describe how amazing he was. I also loved his character and love for Jesus, special qualities in the rough and tumble world of hardworking men.

One day, Richard introduced me to a jackhammer and compressor, and thus I began some of the hardest work I had ever done. We started the engine on the compressor, and I picked up the (extremely heavy) jackhammer and began to break up a huge concrete slab.

After a while, I noticed that once the engine on the compressor had filled the tank with enough pressurized air, it shifted into what sounded like a neutral gear. Simultaneously, there was a loud hissing sound coming from a small valve mounted on the side of the tank. It was releasing air. At the close of the day, as Richard was driving this tired and sore college boy back to the house, I asked him about the hissing sound. He explained that when the tank is filled to capacity with pressurized air, it tells the engine to take a break. "What happens if the pressure valve doesn't let the engine know what's going on inside?" I asked. Richard gave me a wordless smile that conveyed something about "smithereens."

WHEN YOU SPEAK WITH YOUR WIFE ABOUT SOMETHING YOU'RE FACING, A SENSE OF RELIEF WILL USUALLY RESULT.

As a husband, when I am facing any kind of temptation, I have two choices. I can tell my wife about it and release the pressure that's building in my heart. Or I can keep it inside and risk an explosion. When you speak with your wife about something you're facing, a sense of relief will usually result. You might not hear a hissing sound, but your spirit will be lifted.

And you're not the only one who will benefit. When you tell your wife about a temptation you're struggling with, she needs to know
that she has a shepherd—a safe place—to take
her concerns to when she's facing the same

**ADAM HAD A CHANCE
TO STEP UP, STEP IN,
AND SPEAK. HE DIDN'T.**

kind of peril. The Bible tells us that temptation is "common to mankind"
(1 Corinthians 10:13). You and I face temptations that are peculiar to
men, but most temptations do not discriminate on the basis of sex.

Step Up. Step In.
Dare to speak.

When Nancy and I were planning our wedding, an idea flashed
into my head. And to be perfectly honest, Adam was the inspiration.

Nancy's brother and my friend, Mark DeMoss, was going to
escort her down the aisle to her waiting groom. "Why don't you stop
walking when you and Mark get halfway down the aisle," I suggested. "And then I'll come to get you and escort you the rest of the
way to the front of the church." Nancy got it right away, and she liked
the idea—a lot.

I mentioned earlier that Genesis 3:6 indicates that Adam was
probably present when the serpent approached his wife but didn't
speak up when she was tempted. As Eve tottered on the brink of
disaster, her shepherd was standing right there, yet he did nothing.
We don't know if he was as beguiled by the serpent as Eve was or if
he was simply unwilling to displease his wife. It doesn't really matter.
Adam had a chance to step up, step in, and speak. He didn't.

Everything She Needs

Revisiting the opening phrase of Psalm 23, your wife has a Good
Shepherd. He has promised His presence and His protection and His

care. What your wife also needs is an earthly shepherd who is transparent about his own struggles, giving her a window to his heart, a shepherd who steps in, clearly and fearlessly expressing his concerns and warnings.

This "everything" does not come in a brown truck. It cannot be found on the Internet. It is not on display in the showcase of a department store. The "everything" comes to your wife by way of her husband. It's what she needs.

EIGHT

A SHEPHERD LEADS HIS SHEEP

He leads me beside still waters. He restores
my soul. He leads me in paths of righteousness
for his name's sake.

—PSALM 23:2–3

Leadership can be a slippery concept. As we've seen, the hard-driving cowboy is one model, but he's not very effective with sheep, which long to be led. How should we lead in our marriages, taking into account our gifts, skills, and experience? Not every man is a natural-born leader, but every husband is called to "headship":

> For the husband is the head of the wife even as Christ is the head of the church, his body, and is himself its Savior. Now as the church submits to Christ, so also wives should submit in everything to their husbands. (Ephesians 5:23–24)

From these words of Paul and the verses I've quoted above from Psalm 23, it seems that our calling as shepherds entails *who* we are

NOT EVERY MAN IS A NATURAL-BORN LEADER, BUT EVERY HUSBAND IS CALLED TO "HEADSHIP."

and *what* we're supposed to do. We are the head and we are supposed to learn how to lead.

If it's any consolation—and I'm hoping that it is—the Scripture gives us a clear assignment: Be like Jesus. Even for guys like you and me who may have been consigned to the slow reading group in the fourth grade, this is impossible to miss. The Lord *makes* me lie down, He *leads* me, He *restores* my soul, He *leads* me in paths of righteousness. And " ... even *as Christ* is the head of the church."

See Rock City

Do you read bumper stickers? Of course you do. So do I. Some say that bumper stickers originated at the famous Rock City attraction at Lookout Mountain, Georgia, where visitors returned to their cars to find a "See Rock City" sticker applied to their rear bumper—without their permission.

If I were to create a bumper sticker—which I would never apply to your car without asking—it would help husbands think about their leadership and headship in a new way:

What if your wife were married to Jesus?

A Hard Act to Follow

For many of the years that preceded my engagement to Nancy Leigh DeMoss, she wore a lovely ring on the third finger of her left hand, the finger on which people wear wedding bands. When I first saw the ring, I asked about it. She explained that she had worn it for years as a reminder that though she had never married, she belonged to Christ.

Early in her life, she felt the call to ministry as a single woman. A staunch champion of marriage and an encourager and counselor to many married women, Nancy never envisioned herself as a wife. But as a part of the Bride of Christ, she was devoted to love and serve Him with all her heart.

Several months after we began dating, we were having dinner with some close friends of mine, a couple who had known and loved my late wife, Bobbie. After a long and pleasant conversation, the husband was talking about how special Bobbie was, when he turned, looking straight into Nancy's face, and said, "Bobbie's a hard act to follow."

My heart leapt into my throat, and I could feel the color drain from my face. This was one of the most embarrassing moments of my adult life. Yes, of course, Bobbie was special. We had been married almost forty-five years and had a strong and wonderful relationship. Together we had two amazing daughters. Nancy and Bobbie had been friends. But this comment seemed so far out of bounds that a referee would have needed to take a taxicab to make the call. Nancy did not say anything. I didn't either, but for the remainder of the evening the man's comment had its way, grinding in my stomach.

WHAT IF YOUR WIFE WERE MARRIED TO JESUS?

On the drive home, I tried to express to Nancy how terrible I felt about my friend's insensitive comment; Nancy graciously responded that she understood how difficult it must be for longtime friends of Bobbie's to adjust to my having another woman in my life.

The next day, I was on the phone with my daughter Julie, who has always been one step ahead. (She was probably eight years old when she asked me if there was another word for "thesaurus" and why sour cream has an expiration date.) When I told her about the "you've got a hard act to follow" comment, she replied, "Remember, Daddy, Nancy was married to Jesus. And *He's* a hard act to follow!"

AS USEFUL AS OUR GADGETS ARE FOR CALLING UP INFORMATION AND STAYING IN TOUCH WITH PEOPLE, THEY CAN SERIOUSLY DISRUPT OUR REST.

I gave a half-hearted laugh, realizing what a challenge she had just issued.

The Apostle Paul, who instructed the Christian husbands of Ephesus about headship and acting like Jesus, also wrote, "Let each of you look not only to his own interests, but also to the interests of others. Have this mind among yourselves, which is yours in Christ Jesus." (Philippians 2:4–5)

Do you see it? Paul agrees with our bumper sticker. What if your wife were married to Jesus? What would His headship look like? What effect might His leadership, love, and grace have on her spirit, responses, and reactions? Does *your* leadership have the same effect?

All good questions.

He Makes Me Lie Down in Green Pastures

Do you see the strength of the Good Shepherd's directive? Why does He *make* us lie down in green pastures (Psalm 23:2)? Why not just invite us? Or encourage us? Doesn't this sound a little forceful for a shepherd?

I can't wait to answer this question because you and I know that the real skill of leadership is knowing your protégés even better than they know themselves. Jesus, the Good Shepherd, looks at you and me and issues a two-word directive—"Lie down."

Jesus doesn't tell us to "sit," as we would tell our dog when it's time to give him a treat. In our case, sitting isn't going to be enough. We need something else. Something more important. We need rest, and our Shepherd knows it.

Rest may mean a better night's sleep than you're accustomed to. It may require taking time out from your routine for reading your Bible and writing in a journal, recording your thoughts. Rest may mean taking your wife for a long walk or finding a special place where the two of you can talk, unhurried and uninterrupted. Whatever form your "rest" takes, I'm pretty sure that it will require that you take nothing electronic along. As useful as our gadgets are for calling up information and staying in touch with people, they can seriously disrupt our rest.

Father Knows Best

The old sitcom *Father Knows Best* is a symbol of everything the sexual revolution has overturned, a byword for "out of date." Yet the title—now so politically incorrect that it makes us smile—sums up the timeless truth that a dad can be trusted to faithfully shepherd his wife and his family because he "knows best." The same is true of our Shepherd. Because our heavenly Father loves us, He makes us do what He knows is best. In this case, He makes us stop, lie down, and rest.

In 1981, I had just been awarded a promotion in my first book-publishing job. My boss told me that he appreciated my work and thought I could carry greater responsibility. This motivated me to work harder than I had ever worked. I confess that I spent far too much time at the office for a young dad. I was there physically whenever I could be and mentally there the rest of the time. Maybe you've done this.

My daughters, ten and seven, were at an age when they were making decisions and setting patterns that would have a lifetime effect. They had never needed their dad more than they needed him then. My wife did her best to help me. Occasionally, she would bring the girls to the office with a picnic basket, and we'd have dinner on the floor, a red-checked tablecloth spread out on the carpet in front of my desk.

I pressed and pressed, spending the entire night at least once a month, sitting at my desk the day financial reports were distributed. My body began sending reports, too. My appetite waned. I tried to keep up my workout regimen, but found that I was too exhausted. When I competed in a 5K race, I collapsed in a heap at the finish line. I was overwhelmed.

I had a trip to Hawaii scheduled—not a vacation but a business trip. Suspecting that something was wrong with me, I visited the doctor just a few hours before my flight to Honolulu. His nurse drew some blood and promised a report "in a day or two."

The day after I arrived in Hawaii, in the middle of media luncheons and interviews, I was handed a note: "Call your office." When I reached my secretary, she said, "I have booked you on the next flight home. There's a serious problem." Thinking of my wife and two young daughters, I was immediately filled with terror. "What happened?" I demanded. "Is my family okay?"

"Yes," she replied, "But you're not. You have hepatitis." She paused and then repeated, "I have you on the next flight home." Then she added, "If you tell the people there, you may be quarantined and unable to travel. Don't say anything about this to anyone."

> I PRESSED AND PRESSED, SPENDING THE ENTIRE NIGHT AT LEAST ONCE A MONTH, SITTING AT MY DESK THE DAY FINANCIAL REPORTS WERE DISTRIBUTED.

Relieved that the problem was with me rather than with my wife or daughters and grateful to have a diagnosis, I caught my flight home. Soon I was sitting on the crinkly paper-covered examining table in my doctor's office, my naked legs dangling in midair. He was not happy with me for having taken the trip feeling so sick, repeating what my secretary had said:

"Good thing you didn't tell anyone you had hepatitis." And then he pulled a pen from his pocket, wrote out a prescription, and handed it to me. I was shocked to see but a single word—"Rest." In spite of his doctoresque penmanship, I could read it. Clearly.

> LIKE A GOOD SHEPHERD, LIKE *THE* GOOD SHEPHERD, MY PHYSICIAN WAS MAKING—*MAKING*—ME LIE DOWN.

I looked at him, thinking this was some kind of joke. "Rest?" I asked.

"Yes," he said. "In spite of the fact that this is a dangerous condition, there is nothing I can give you. No medication. No pills. The only thing you can do to get well is…nothing." I argued, trying to explain that I was too busy to stop. There was a sales conference to prepare for, and another big book was about to be released. My doctor was not listening.

Like a good shepherd, like *the* Good Shepherd, my physician was making—*making*—me lie down. This was the voice I needed to hear. And my doctor's directive, though simple, was the right prescription.

So our Good Shepherd has told us—ordered us—to lie down. To stop. To rest.

And since you and I are in shepherd school, learning from the example of our Good Shepherd, I wonder if this message is also for our wives. Yes, I think it is. And the Lord is asking us to follow His example and ask our wives to rest.

The Joy of Serving

It's likely that if you told your wife about her Good Shepherd's admonition to "lie down in green pastures," she'd respond just as I did when my doctor gave me the prescription to rest. If your kids are at home, this may be the busiest, most strenuous time of her life. As an unknown bard (almost certainly a woman) wrote, "Man may work from sun to sun, but a woman's work is never done."

She may not be a professional juggler, but with all that she has to do, she'd qualify. As her shepherd, it's your responsibility—and joy—to "make" her rest. And the fun of this comes when she gives you that "How am I going to do this?" look, the one that needs no caption, and you simply answer, "Is there anything I can do for you?"

The final two and a half years of my almost forty-five-year marriage to Bobbie were our best two and a half years. She thought so. I thought so. And our daughters would agree. Undergoing six multiple-infusion rounds of chemotherapy, Bobbie needed a lot of rest. And even though she spent most of this time active and pain-free, I had the joy of serving her in a way that I hadn't ever done before.

> **AS HER SHEPHERD, IT'S YOUR RESPONSIBILITY—AND JOY—TO "MAKE" HER REST.**

It's not that I had been parked on the couch with something cold in my hand for four decades, but let's just say I hadn't *always* followed my father's exhortation, repeated constantly throughout my childhood, "Look for something to do." Even though Bobbie had always been grateful for the things I did around the house, it wasn't until 2012, when her doctor told us we were facing Stage IV ovarian cancer that I really began to "look for something to do."

And here's the kicker: I was never happier in my marriage than in those final two and a half years of Bobbie's life. Making early-morning oatmeal just the way she liked it, washing and folding the laundry, and driving her to her treatments brought me pure joy. And please don't give me a bit of credit for this. Jesus' words "It is more blessed to give than receive" (Acts 20:35) reflect a simple truth about human nature—we are happiest when we serve.

Picking Up the Tab

If you have ever surprised your friends by stealthily picking up the check at a restaurant before they have a chance to argue with you about it, you know the delight of generosity. Our Good Shepherd has "ordered" us to rest. He knows what's best. And you and I have been given the joy of "making" our wife rest, doing everything we can to make that happen because we know she needs it.

One of my favorite characters in the Bible is Joshua, who led the Israelites into the Promised Land after forty years of wandering in the wilderness. I used to assume that the primary reason they were so excited about entering Canaan was God's description of it as a "land flowing with milk and honey." It is true that God's promise included material prosperity, but there was more.

In Joshua's final speech to God's chosen people before entering the Promised Land, he told them, "Remember the word that Moses the servant of the LORD commanded you, saying, 'The LORD your God is providing you a place of rest and will give you this land.'" (Joshua 1:13) After centuries of slavery, travel, disruption, chaos, and pain, God was giving His people a homeland so they could rest.

My friend, Pastor Trent Griffith points out that Joshua went on to explain who was to benefit from this rest: "Your wives, your little ones, and your livestock shall remain in the land that Moses gave you beyond the Jordan.... " (Joshua 1:14) God gave the Promised Land to the Israelites so they could provide rest and security for their wives and their families and even their animals.

We are responsible for taking our wives to a place where they can rest, just as our Shepherd takes us to the same place. We have been called to this responsibility by virtue of our marriage, so we don't need to ask permission to do this. You're the man. I am as well.

That Headship Thing . . . Again

Before moving on, I want to make sure that the responsibility of "headship" is clear. It goes without saying that this concept is openly scorned in our culture. Why? Because when folks are uninformed about the admonitions of God's Word, their stereotypes of male leadership or headship take them to a place that God never intended. Actually, we have Archie Bunker to thank for this.

WE ARE RESPONSIBLE FOR TAKING OUR WIVES TO A PLACE WHERE THEY CAN REST.

Archie was a caricature—a thoughtless jerk, a loud-mouthed chauvinist, a cleverly-designed foil for the growing feminist movement in the 1970s. America laughed as a bloated and rude Archie sat in his chair, insulting his son-in-law, belittling his wife, and generally bellowing bigotry. *All in the Family*'s attack on the biblical concept of male headship was cloaked in sitcom humor. No decent man would ever embrace Archie as his role model, but he represented "traditional" manhood. Viewers laughed at the ridiculous patriarch, the head of the house and the butt of the jokes.

When *All in the Family* finished its run in 1979, not one woman in America longed to be the pathetic Edith, married to such a thoughtless oaf. And like a man who walks away from an argument without speaking or making his point, Christian men who failed to denounce Archie's foolishness allowed the world to assume that his not-so-subtle assumptions about what the head of the home looked like were correct. Talk about a "hard act to follow"!

So what is the antidote for Archie Bunker? Do you remember the account in the Bible of when James and John approached Jesus asking "to sit, one at your right hand and one at your left, in glory" (Mark 10:37)? Jesus responded:

You know that those who are considered rulers of the Gentiles lord it over them, and their great ones exercise authority over them. But it shall not be so among you. But whoever would be great among you must be your servant, and whoever would be first among you must be slave of all. Even the Son of Man came not to be served but to serve, and to give his life as a ransom for many. (Mark 10:42–45)

It's as if Jesus said to us, "So you want to be the head of your marriage? That's good. It's what I want you to do. It's an admirable goal. Then serve your wife with all your heart. Take the authority that's yours and love her well, just as I have loved you."

> "SO YOU WANT TO BE THE HEAD OF YOUR MARRIAGE? THAT'S GOOD. IT'S WHAT I WANT YOU TO DO. IT'S AN ADMIRABLE GOAL. THEN SERVE YOUR WIFE WITH ALL YOUR HEART."

Remember that car show I visited with my son-in-law and teenage grandsons? And remember the way it felt for me to sit behind the wheel of a Bentley? The leather smell was almost intoxicating. But lovingly shepherding your wife makes this euphoric experience in an exotic car look like test-driving a used tricycle. Leading her with love and grace is incomparable to anything you could drive—or do.

NINE

A Shepherd Protects His Sheep

Your wife is surrounded by predators, some of whom are visible. She knows this, which is why she is probably the one who makes sure that your doors are locked when you go to bed each night. You are a sentinel, gun on your shoulder, pacing back and forth on the top of the wall—a shepherd packing heat. But most of the dangers your wife faces can't be seen.

> Behold, the Lord GOD comes with might, and his arm rules for him.... He will feed his flock like a shepherd, he will gather the lambs in his arms, he will carry them in his bosom, and gently lead those that are with young. (Isaiah 40:10–11)

YOU ARE A SENTINEL, GUN ON SHOULDER, PACING BACK AND FORTH ON THE TOP OF THE WALL—A SHEPHERD PACKING HEAT.

Do you love this image as much as I do? The Lord God, our Good Shepherd, is not lacking in any way. His arms are strong. And in His tenderness, He scoops us up in those arms and carries us, protects us, and gently leads us.

You don't need to look long or far to find a wonderful illustration of what this looks like for you and your wife. It's one of the most tender love stories in your Bible. It's a true story of a husband who had this kind of heart.

Boaz and Ruth

Family vacations when Missy and Julie were young provided us with memories to last our lifetimes. A week away from the daily grind always provided us with new experiences and lots of time to be together. It was Bobbie's idea for the family to read a book of the Bible during our time together. One year we read the story of Ruth and Boaz, a love story of the highest order. Do you remember how it goes?

A famine in Judah drove a woman called Naomi, her husband, and their two sons into the land of Moab. Naomi's husband soon died, and her sons married Moabite girls, Orpah and Ruth. Then, before either marriage had produced offspring, both sons followed their father to the grave.

When word reached Moab that the famine in Judah had come to an end, Naomi decided to return home. But she urged her Moabite daughters-in-law to stay among their own people rather than travel with her to a foreign land. With tears, Orpah agreed to stay, "but Ruth clung to her," declaring her fealty to her mother-in-law in one of the most beautiful passages in the Bible:

Entreat me not to leave you or to return from following you; for where you go I will go, and where you lodge I will lodge; your people shall be my people, and your God my God; where you die I will die, and there will I be buried. May the LORD do so to me and more also if even death parts me from you. (Ruth 1:16–17)

And so with all their earthly possessions on their backs, the two destitute widows made the seven-to-ten-day journey to Bethlehem, Naomi's hometown. It was harvest time, and upon their arrival, the enterprising Ruth gleaned in a barley field after the harvesters to provide food for herself and her mother-in-law. While Ruth was gleaning, the owner of the field arrived, a kinsman of Naomi's husband named Boaz. "The LORD be with you!" he called out to the reapers. "The LORD bless you," they replied—an exchange that indicated Boaz's unusual kindness to his bond-slaves. Imagine the humble and hungry Ruth, bent over as she gathers loose stalks of barley, hearing the landowner's voice and witnessing the workers' response to him.

Boaz noticed a stranger among the young women in the field. Told that she was Naomi's daughter-in-law, he approached her and said,

Now, listen, my daughter, do not go to glean in another field or leave this one, but keep close to my young women. Let your eyes be on the field that they are reaping, and go after them. Have I not charged the young men not to touch you? And when you are thirsty, go to the vessels and drink what the young men have drawn. (2:8–9)

Overwhelmed, Ruth bowed low and softly said, "Why such goodness, my lord?"

"I heard of the kindness you have shown the widow Naomi," Boaz said. "May the Lord repay you for what you have done. May you be richly rewarded by the Lord, the God of Israel, under whose wings you have come to take refuge." (2:11–12, paraphrased)

"May I find favor in your eyes, my lord." Captivated by his manners and gentleness, Ruth continued, "You have put me at ease by speaking kindly—though I do not have the standing of one of your servants." (2:13) Boaz was attentive to the new worker, and later, at mealtime, he offered Ruth as much roasted grain as she could eat. Then he told his men to watch over her and to drop plenty of stalks in her path.

When Ruth returned to her mother-in-law at the end of the day and told her about the gracious man named Boaz, Naomi exclaimed, "The Lord bless him! God has not stopped his kindness to us.... That man is our close relative; he is one of our guardian-redeemers." (2:20 NIV)

A Good Shepherd

She might have said, "Boaz is a good shepherd—our good shepherd—and he has chosen to care for his own."

The next day Ruth returned to the same field and worked under Boaz's protection. She gathered a bountiful supply of grain every day for two more months. And then the harvest season ended. "Now, it is time to find a home for you," Naomi said to Ruth. "I think Boaz is the man who could provide what you need."

Ruth listened carefully as Naomi continued. "Boaz will be winnowing barley on the threshing floor tonight. Wash and perfume yourself, put on your best clothes and go. Do not let him know you are there. Wait until he eats and falls asleep and then lie down at his feet, covering yourself with the hem of his garment. He will know what to do when he awakes." (3:1–4 NIV)

Ruth did as Naomi instructed. During the night, Boaz stirred and awakened. Seeing someone lying at his feet, he asked "Who are you?"

"I am your servant, Ruth," she replied softly, her heart racing with expectation and fear. "With the corner of your garment please cover me. You are a guardian-redeemer of our family." (3:9 NIV)

"The Lord bless you my daughter," Boaz replied. "You have not run after the younger men. Don't be afraid, my daughter; I will do for you as you asked." Boaz would take Ruth as his wife. God had provided.

I think I know how Boaz must have felt when he first saw Ruth. After my first wife died, my heart was drawn to Nancy, and as she received my acts of kindness and the interest I showed her, Nancy responded gratefully and humbly; these words expressed her heart toward me. "Why have I found favor in your eyes, that you should take notice of me, since I am a foreigner?" (2:10)

Early in our courtship, Nancy began to read this story in her daily Bible reading. It was one she had studied and taught many times throughout her years of ministry as a single woman. But given my expressed love for her and my pursuit of her heart, this account took on new meaning. Often she would close her text messages with "YVOR"—your very own Ruth.

Protection

The moment I saw my first daughter in September 1971—so tiny and beautiful and defenseless—I thought, "I'm your daddy, and although I have no idea what I'm doing here, I'm going to protect you." As she grew, my role as my daughter's protector shifted from protecting her little body to protecting her heart. When she was tiny and portable, she needed physical protection. As she grew and was able to take care of her body, her need for protection became less visible, more emotional and spiritual.

I loved this role, and now that Missy and Julie are married and have wonderful husbands and growing children of their own, my investment in their lives when they were small has paid sweet dividends. We consider each other among our closest friends.

In our dangerous world, protecting your children is a no-brainer. The neighbor's snarling dog and a teenage boy's furtive glances make a daddy necessary. But how does a husband protect his wife?

> IN OUR DANGEROUS WORLD, PROTECTING YOUR CHILDREN IS A NO-BRAINER. THE NEIGHBOR'S SNARLING DOG AND A TEENAGE BOY'S FURTIVE GLANCES MAKE A DADDY NECESSARY. BUT HOW DOES A HUSBAND PROTECT HIS WIFE?

Physical Protection

If you Google the phrase "Old School," my name may come up. I know that not every wife appreciates the kinds of things that I have done as a husband, but because I grew up watching a dad who was a gentleman, these things come naturally. And I believe that they have been pleasing to my wife. Things like ...

Taking Her Hand...Giving Her My Arm...Opening the Door ...

As I said, this stuff is old school. And your wife may think it's silly and archaic.

When I am walking down the sidewalk with my wife, I always walk on the street side. The tradition dates back to horse-and-buggy days, when wagon wheels would hit mud puddles and splash the dirty water on pedestrians. There also was the occasional runaway horse.

But even though there are not many buggies traveling on the roads where we live, I still do this. I do not make a big deal of it. In fact, I'm not sure if I've ever mentioned it. I just always slip to the street side—the more dangerous side—when we're walking.

When we arrive somewhere in the car, my wife waits for me to open the door and help her out. I do the same when we're leaving our garage, helping her step into the passenger side. One rainy day I was helping Nancy into the car. When she stepped onto the running board, her foot slipped. Because I had taken her arm, she slipped but did not fall to the ground. Yes, she did have a small bruise on her shin, but my hand steadied her and she stayed upright. When I made my way to the driver's side and sat down, Nancy reached over, took my hand, and thanked me. That was it. Not a big deal, but I was glad I was there to protect her from falling.

But as with my daughters, the protection of my wife includes the less tangible kind.

Emotional Protection

One day I could tell Nancy was struggling. I didn't know what was troubling her, but the downcast look on her face was a clue. "What's up? Are you okay?" I asked with a look of sincere interest on my face. Nancy had told me the adage that there are four things that make people vulnerable to temptation: hunger, anger, loneliness, and tiredness. (You can remember that by the acronym HALT.) She admitted that, at that moment, she was feeling hungry and tired. I encouraged her to take a rest—she had stayed up all night writing—and when she awoke, I heated up a bowl of chicken chili and served her. There was no flourish or pomp. Just a simple bowl of chili.

Before we crawled into bed that night, she thanked me for taking care of her needs. I told her this was my great joy, because it was.

Relationship Dangers

Quite early in our courtship, Nancy told me about an ongoing struggle she had in a particular relationship. She knew I was listening because I asked questions as she spoke. How long has this been going on? Have there been sweet times in the relationship? What happened to break this down? What have you done to try to restore it? Are you praying for this person?

BEFORE WE CRAWLED INTO BED THAT NIGHT, SHE THANKED ME FOR TAKING CARE OF HER NEEDS. I TOLD HER THIS WAS MY GREAT JOY, BECAUSE IT WAS.

When she was finished, I told her that, as her friend, I was committed to standing with her. "Your struggles in this situation are my struggles too," I said. Since we were riding in the car and had some uninterrupted time, I offered to take a minute to pray for her and this problem. In my prayer, I repeated what I had said about my willingness to join Nancy in carrying this burden with her. That was it. There was no three-point sermon or ongoing explanation. I did my best to empathize and then asked the Lord for wisdom in coming alongside. Nancy says this was one of those not-be-forgotten times early in our relationship.

Feeling Safe

Your intentional protection of your wife will make her feel safe. If you ask a shepherd, he'll tell you that helping his sheep feel a sense of safety is a high priority.

But let's be honest about this. No matter how much physical or emotional protection you try to provide, your efforts will fall short—always. The good news, though, is that it's not up to you: "God is our refuge and strength, a very present help in trouble." (Psalm 46:1)

On our kitchen counter sits a plaque with a familiar verse from the Old Testament: "The eternal God is your dwelling place, and underneath are the everlasting arms." (Deuteronomy 33:27) Text messaging each other late at night from remote locations became a habit early in my friendship with Nancy. And because I knew how much she appreciated the verse above, I would often text her a blessing: "May you rest safely in our Good Shepherd's Arms."

My first marriage began on March 28, 1970. I was twenty-two years old. Bobbie was twenty. We were kids. And over the next forty-four and a half years, we grew up. We discovered each other's longings and dreams. And we learned about each other's apprehensions and fears. I found great satisfaction helping my wife to realize her dreams, and I loved protecting her when she was afraid.

When we received her cancer diagnosis early in 2012, we told each other that we were not angry. We were not afraid. Those Good Shepherd's arms held us safely.

On October 28, 2014, I sent this email to family and close friends: "This morning at 10:50 EDT, Bobbie stepped into heaven. Missy and Julie were here, so the four of us were able to experience this miracle together. For the past fifteen years or so, every time one of us arrives safely after a flight or a long road trip, we text one word to each other. 'Safe.' Now our Bobbie is safe."

I FOUND GREAT SATISFACTION HELPING MY WIFE TO REALIZE HER DREAMS, AND I LOVED PROTECTING HER WHEN SHE WAS AFRAID.

When Nancy and I were married in November 2015, we were not kids. But we are quickly discovering each other's longings and dreams. And we are learning each other's apprehensions and fears. As I did for almost forty-five years with Bobbie, I am finding great satisfaction helping Nancy to realize her dreams, and I love protecting her when she is afraid or uncertain or anxious. Like Bobbie—and

AS LONG AS I WAS
PHYSICALLY ABLE,
I DID NOT WANT A
STRANGER—TRAINED
THOUGH SHE MAY BE—
TO CARE FOR THIS LAMB.

probably your wife—Nancy also longed to be safe.

The Valley of the Shadow of Death

"Even though I walk through the valley of the shadow of death, I will fear no evil, for you are with me…" (Psalm 23:4).

In the fall of 2014, the shadow of death lengthened. As Bobbie grew weaker and weaker, I had the joy of being her caregiver. Missy and Julie flew to Orlando a few times for a few days so I could rest a bit, but it was my primary responsibility to be her shepherd as never before.

We did have the option of hiring a round-the-clock nurse, but Bobbie was my wife, my charge. As long as I was physically able, I did not want a stranger—trained though she may be—to care for this lamb. This would be my privilege. From the time she was twenty years old, I had been her earthly shepherd. Forty-four years later, with the encouragement of friends, I decided I would not walk away from this opportunity to care for her as long as I could.

Normally, I do not use an alarm clock to wake up in the morning, but during the weeks I cared for Bobbie in her illness, I learned how to set the ringer on my smartphone for every four hours. And sometimes the electronic chirp woke me from the depths, even though I had been sleeping only a few hours. I was indescribably tired, but the size of the task inspired me.

For You Are with Me

On the afternoon of Monday, October 27, 2014, Missy and Julie arrived in Orlando. They knew that the purpose of this trip was to say good-bye to their mother. She knew it as well. The next few hours were unforgettable. Bobbie, completely lucid and alert, was thrilled to have Missy and Julie there. We talked. We laughed. We cried. We remembered.

At 8:30, I went to our bedroom, perhaps more exhausted than I had ever been in my life. Ninety minutes later, Missy gently woke me up, doing her best not to startle me. "Mom is calling for you," she said. We had just twelve more hours with Bobbie. During the short time I had slept, Bobbie told her Missy and Julie, "I'm going to die tomorrow. I'm going to see Jesus soon." She also reported seeing "white twinkle lights everywhere."

For the rest of the night, Missy, Julie, and I made camp in the living room around Bobbie's hospital bed. But even though she was inching toward the finish line, almost too weak to move on her own, she insisted with a wry smile on handling the hospital-bed controls. This gave all four of us something to laugh about.

At 10:20 the next morning, Enid, our hospice nurse, arrived. "Hello, Miss Bobbie," she said sweetly.

"Hello, Enid," Bobbie replied, opening her arms to welcome a hug.

Enid went quickly about her work, putting the blood pressure cuff on Bobbie's upper arm. Bobbie made it easy, raising her right arm in the air. Listening carefully through her stethoscope, Enid pumped the rubber bulb and then let out the air. She pumped it again, letting the air out with a soft hiss.

"What's the matter?" Bobbie asked, seeing the look on the nurse's face.

"Your blood pressure is 80 over 40," she said.

"That's low, isn't it?" Bobbie replied.

"Yes, Miss Bobbie, that's very low."

Enid then took Bobbie's right wrist to capture her pulse. She was quiet and did not move. Missy, Julie, and I did not speak. Then Enid reached over to Bobbie's other wrist, but again said nothing. "You can't find a pulse, can you?" Bobbie asked.

"No, Miss Bobbie, I can't."

Then Bobbie asked us if we could help her roll over on her right side toward me. I was seated, which put our faces at the same level. Bobbie reached out with both of her hands and took me by the shirt, drawing my face to within a few inches of hers. Completely alert, she spoke clearly: "I love you so much." With that she let go of my shirt and stepped into heaven.

Shocked by the suddenness of what had just happened, Missy asked Enid, "Is she dying?"

"Yes, she is," the nurse replied with the steadiness of a professional.

We rolled my wife onto her back. Enid laid her hand on Bobbie's chest for a lingering moment. "There's no breathing. There's no heartbeat. She's gone."

Thank You for Letting Me Be Your Shepherd

We called the funeral home where we had already made arrangements. Enid went about her paperwork duties. Missy, Julie, and I sat quietly around the hospital bed that had held Bobbie but now held only her body. I took her hand. Her face slowly grew gray and chilled.

In those moments I thanked the Lord for this woman. For her love for Jesus and for loving her family. And I thanked her for the privilege of being her earthly shepherd for all these years.

The only way to describe these moments would be to say that they were sacred. We will never forget them.

In his book, *Seven Habits of Highly Effective People*, bestselling author Stephen Covey invites you to imagine your own wake, to listen to what people say as they pass by your coffin as you lie in state. But if I may, I'd like to suggest an even more powerful, if painful, exercise of the imagination. You are a shepherd. Your wife is your charge, your lamb. If she were dead, as Bobbie was, and you had to look back on how you fulfilled your responsibilities for her, what would you think?

What would you wish you had done better? What would you wish you had not done? As you look back over your life together, what are some of the really happy memories? Where could you have done a better job of loving her?

Now you can wake up. Your wife, your lamb, is alive. There's still time for you to recommit yourself to your role as her shepherd. Is there anything hindering your fulfillment of this responsibility? This privilege? This joy?

And to ask you one more question: What is keeping you from stepping up? Nothing? Good. God bless you, Mr. Shepherd.

TEN

A SHEPHERD COMFORTS HIS SHEEP

Your rod and your staff, they comfort me.
—PSALM 23:4

To understand what the Psalmist means when he writes that the Shepherd "comforts" His sheep, let's take a run at another activity that takes place out in a field—baseball.

America's Pastime

Some think that baseball is called America's pastime because of its slow pace. "You can sure pass a lot of time watching it." But not for me. I love baseball.

As a kid I could not pass a field where the game was being played without stopping. Baseball was the only sport I tried out for in high school. I did not make the team. But this did not diminish my affection for the game. As a teenager in the Chicago area, my team of

ONE OF THE GREAT
THEOLOGICAL TRUTHS
FOUND IN THE BIBLE
IS THAT JESUS, OUR
SHEPHERD, RUNS FROM
THE DUGOUT AND STANDS
BEFORE GOD THE FATHER
TO PLEAD OUR CASE.

choice was the Cubs, who, in 2016, after a 108-year drought, won the World Series. In fact, my favorite dog—a little white Maltese—was named Wrigley.

As a grown-up, I have enjoyed friendships with a few professional baseball players, from whom I learned some of the secrets of the game—the "chatter" that takes place on the field, the subtle hand gestures, the head nods, and facial expressions. But what makes me think of baseball right now is not the players or the strategy. It's the managers. And the umpires.

Subjectivity Reigns

Until recently, there was no video review in baseball, no impromptu conclaves of umpires on the field waiting for other, invisible umpires in a booth somewhere in New York to study the replay, trying to figure out what just happened. I don't like video review in baseball. I actually prefer the subjectivity.

The home-plate umpire's calling balls and strikes all on his own adds to the fascination of the game. In fact, if the manager shouts challenges to the call from the dugout, he can be ejected from the game. No jury. No judge. No trial. Straight to the showers. The umpire, as they say, "calls 'em as he sees 'em."

And what does the manager do when one of these "borderline" calls goes against his player? He storms out of the dugout and makes his way to the offending umpire, giving him the original "in your face" treatment. Red-hot with anger, the manager jaws at the umpire, who jaws right back. Perhaps the manager, having exhausted his repertoire of insults and profanities, finishes by kicking dirt on the umpire's glossy black shoes. The hometown folks love this, cheering for more like the crowd at a gladiator fight. When the umpire has had enough, he ejects the manager from the game.

What's the point? There has been no resolution. No resolve. No "meeting of the minds." No matter how many games you watch, in these subjective, non-video replay decisions, you'll never see an umpire change his call. The manager loses the argument every time. So why does he bother? He does it, I believe, for the benefit of the player who has been called out at the plate—it's how the manager comforts him.

Here's what I mean. Even though the umpire's authority is absolute, even though the call will not be reversed, even though the manager is going to make a fool of himself in front of all these people, even though he's going to get ejected and handed a stiff fine, what he does on his player's behalf earns that player's respect. It gives him confidence. This scene, silly though it may seem, brings that player comfort.

One of the great theological truths found in the Bible is that Jesus, our Shepherd, runs from the dugout and stands before God the Father to plead our case. "My little children, I am writing these things to you so that you may not sin. But if anyone does sin, we have an advocate with the Father, Jesus Christ the righteous." (1 John 2:1)

However, unlike the baseball manager, our advocate is the sinless Son of God. But the picture of this Shepherd defending us before a Holy God is exactly right. As someone has said, Jesus keeps a photo of you on his smartphone, and when anyone asks Him about you, He proudly displays your likeness and declares that you're His son. That's beyond logic or comprehension, but it's true.

The Rod

In Psalm 23's depiction of our Good Shepherd, there are two things He has with Him at all times. The first is a rod—a short, thick piece of wood with a grip, like the nightstick hanging from a policeman's belt.

The rod is a tool to help the shepherd count his sheep. As when you run your finger along a line of print to help you keep your place, the shepherd uses the rod as a marker that his sheep pass under. The shepherd in the story of the lost sheep may have used the rod to discover that one was missing.

The rod is also a formidable weapon against predators. Just as a baseball player knows that his manager will, if necessary, go after an umpire who makes a bad call—although thankfully without a rod in his hand—there's comfort for a sheep in knowing that her shepherd is armed, ready and willing to defend her.

In the last chapter, we talked about a shepherd's responsibility to protect his sheep. The threat may come from wolves or thieves. You can ask your wife about this, but your willingness to protect her from any kind of outside foe brings her a strong sense of comfort. Sometimes, however, the threat isn't from the outside. Sometimes your wife needs protection from her own children.

SHE HAD CONFRONTED OUR DAUGHTER THAT DAY, AND THE RESULTS WERE DREADFUL. I WAS STANDING UP FOR MY WIFE. AND IN MY STANDING UP FOR HER, SHE WAS COMFORTED.

When my daughter Missy entered the fifth grade, she seemed to change overnight. She started questioning her mother's judgment and came to the conclusion that homework was voluntary. Her once tidy bedroom looked like a fraternity house rec room after a party. But the most troubling change was how she spoke to her mother. The docile and respectful little girl we had known turned on her heel, deciding that her mother was fair game.

One autumn afternoon, Bobbie called me at work. She was deeply troubled about Missy's behavior and attitude. Missy's teacher, Bobbie told me, had called to report on our daughter. In a few minutes, I was standing in Missy's room. She was face down on her bed, but she was not crying. She was too defiant to cry.

With little emotion but plenty of fatherly resolve, I spoke.

"Your mother and I do not know what's up with you, but we know that you're in trouble at school. I have seen the way you are treating your mother...the unacceptable way that you speak to her. And, Melissa Christine, I want you to know something. I will not allow this behavior to continue."

I was not finished.

"You may think you'll win this one. You may think you're going to be able to have your own way here and that we'll just let this go. I love you, but I'm here to tell you something you already know. You will not win. Your dad will win. I promise."

Missy looked up. She may have wanted to see if I was serious about my vow. She saw that I was not kidding. At this, my stiff-necked daughter began to cry. I quickly went to her and sat on the edge of her bed. I leaned down and hugged her. And held her.

Now, you may think this story is about Missy. You may conclude that I'm going to take this moment to give you a few tips on raising an adolescent daughter. But I'm not. This is a story about my wife. It's about her overhearing my stout admonition to our daughter, whose open defiance of her mother alerted me to step in. Could my wife have done this on her own? Of course. She had confronted our daughter that day, and the results were dreadful. I was standing up for my wife. And in my standing up for her, she was comforted.

By the way, if you knew Missy today, you'd have a hard time believing this story. This capable woman has a tender spirit and servant's heart. But during Missy's defiant spell, her mother was a sheep, and I was her shepherd-defender. Bobbie was standing on the base line after a bad call, and I was her manager.

The Rod That Our Good Shepherd Uses

When we were children, we looked for allies who were bigger and stronger than we were. You can remember arguments you had with the neighbor boys. When these fights reached the point where you knew that you were out-numbered or out-classed, you reached out for someone bigger—probably your dad.

You're a grown man now, and your dad may not be able to help you, but there are still times when you need the help of someone stronger or smarter. Admitting that you need help isn't easy. Professionally, I understand this truth.

Working in the same industry for decades, I developed an expertise that reliably put me in a strong place at the conference table discussing book publishing and marketing. Then along came technology and the digital age, and I was looking into the faces of young men and women, just a bit older than my grandchildren, who were talking circles around me. All my years of experience suddenly counted for very little. Confessing my insufficiency has become a lifestyle. In fact, the older I get, the more aware I am of my inabilities and my need for help. Once I felt invincible in my profession. Now I often feel overwhelmed.

Asking for Help

The story of the wandering sheep and the faithful shepherd who drops everything to search for it reminds me of how much I need a Shepherd. My mismatched encounters with technology are nothing compared with the inadequacies I feel in my personal life. That's why I love the Old Testament story of Nehemiah.

About 450 years before Christ, Nehemiah, a Jew in Babylon, was the wine taster for the king of Persia, who valued Nehemiah's advice and counsel. News came to Nehemiah that the walls surrounding Jerusalem had been destroyed. Broken-hearted, he decided to approach the king for help. But first, realizing that the task ahead was well beyond his own capability, he fasted and prayed. This was Nehemiah's habit. He saw a need, realized his own insufficiency, and prayed. He knew that his Shepherd had the power and the will to help him.

> MY GOOD SHEPHERD WAS ABLE TO SAVE ME. I FELT HIS PRESENCE. IT WAS SOMETHING I HAD NEVER EXPERIENCED BEFORE QUITE LIKE THIS.

When I lost my wife to cancer, the loneliness, darkness, and silence of my home was a dark blanket thrown over my soul. I was living in unfamiliar territory. Yes, my family and friends reached out as best they could. Their calls and text messages were encouraging. But these people could not help at the level I needed help. As much as I loved them and as sincere as their expressions of support were, these people simply could not provide what I needed. Then along came my friend Nehemiah. His example of brokenness, need, and constant prayer were my lifeline.

And so I asked for help in a way that I had never asked for it before. Any spiritual self-sufficiency I had known before came to an end. I needed the safety of a strong advocate, a Shepherd with a special expertise in comforting my aching heart.

In a more earnest early-morning time of Bible reading, prayer, and journaling than I had ever known, I found the comfort I needed. My Good Shepherd was able to save me. I felt His presence. It was something I had never experienced before quite like this.

The Staff

In my years of construction work, I have collected quite an array of tools. Some of these are power tools, others require no electricity or gasoline. A shepherd carries only two tools—a rod and a staff. As I've said, the rod helps the shepherd count his sheep and keeps away predators. The sheep are comforted because their shepherd knows them and is willing to fight for their safety.

The staff, a long, slender stick with a hook on one end, is always at the ready. The shepherd selects it with care, smoothing, shaping, and cutting it for his personal use. He uses the staff as a walking stick as he traverses the rocky terrain, leaning on it for support and strength. But the primary use of the staff is to help the shepherd manage his flock.[1]

As a waiter in a fine restaurant uses that little scoop to clear the breadcrumbs from your linen tablecloth, a shepherd uses his staff to gently corral his sheep. With the hooked end he can reach out and catch individual sheep, young or old, and draw them close to himself for careful examination. It is useful for the timid sheep that sometimes kept its distance from the shepherd. The staff is also used for guiding sheep into a new path or through a gate or along dangerous, difficult routes. The staff is usually light, slender, and delicate, never used to punish, always to guide.

Like you and me, sheep often get themselves into dangerous situations. One shepherd wrote that he had seen his own sheep, eager for one more mouthful of fresh grass, climb down steep cliffs, where they slipped and fell into the sea. Like a golfer with one of those extendable ball retrievers, his long staff could lift them out of the water back onto solid ground. If a sheep got stuck fast in labyrinths of wild roses or brambles, and if the thorns were so hooked in their wool they could not possibly pull free, tug as they might, the staff in the hands of a skillful shepherd could free them from their entanglement.

What Happened to the Truck?

In his helpful little book *Ten Questions Every Husband Should Ask His Wife Every Year*, Dr. Tom Elliff tells how he was rear-ended at a stop sign one morning by a young woman in a pickup truck. No one was hurt, but both vehicles were badly damaged, and Tom let the woman use his cellphone to call her husband.

Sobbing, the wife told her husband about the accident and how the "nice man" she had hit was letting her use his phone. *Buddy*, Tom was thinking, *this is your moment. Right now you have an incredible opportunity to speak love, understanding, and encouragement to your wife. Say the right thing and you will reveal the kind of love that captures the heart of every woman. Don't blow it!*

The husband's response was so loud that Tom could hear it clearly: "What happened to the truck?" In a moment, that man—that shepherd—could have used his curved staff to rescue his wife, to calm her spirit, and to reassure her that she was far more precious to him than a hunk of steel and chrome. He could have comforted his wife. But he didn't.

Guardrails

The idea of using a shepherd's staff with your wife could make you a little nervous, and she might find it outrageous. But that's only if you assume that she's a wandering soul, foolishly risking her safety and unable to cordon herself in.

The Lord has blessed me with not just one but *two* extremely bright and capable wives. So who do I think I am suggesting that they need a shepherd with a staff in his hand? That's a good question, an important question. The answer, in my opinion, is straightforward and irrefutable.

Both of these gifted women were grateful for a husband who was a shepherd with a staff in his hand. This was not my idea, it was theirs, inspired by what they believed God's Word said about their relationship to their husband. I did not—would not—force them to let me be their shepherd. Using the Bible as their guide, they made this decision quite on their own, without pressure from me.

Bobbie lovingly referred to my leadership in our relationship as "guardrails." Nancy loves the image of the staff-brandishing "shepherd." This was their choice. And if your wife has made the same

BOBBIE LOVINGLY
REFERRED TO MY
LEADERSHIP IN OUR
RELATIONSHIP AS
"GUARDRAILS." NANCY
LOVES THE IMAGE OF
THE STAFF-BRANDISHING
"SHEPHERD." THIS
WAS THEIR CHOICE.

choice, you have been handed a staff. If this makes you feel just a bit—or a lot—insecure, that's good, because from a human perspective, you don't have the chops to do this at all, much less do it well. To quote a few truth-filled cliches, you are out of your league, over your skis. You've bitten off more than you can chew.

So what are we to do? We follow the clear example set for us.

You and I are sheep. We look to our Shepherd, "the Author and the Finisher of our faith" (Hebrews 12:2) to wield the rod and use the staff. What he does with us and for us, we have the responsibility to do with and for our wives. If she has chosen to let you lead, you have no choice but to do this well...by God's power and in His Spirit.

Impossible

But what if your wife has no interest in letting you lead? Even though she's a fine person, agreeing to your role as "head" in your marriage seems like a mountain too steep to climb. You may even think of her submitting to you in a biblical way as impossible. Yet humble and servant-hearted "headship" is not optional equipment in your marriage. It's comes standard. This responsibility and privilege has belonged to husbands since the beginning of time. God's Word affirms this as truth.

But if your wife is not interested in submitting, you can't talk her into it. If she has made up her mind, you cannot change it. Years ago, I heard a marriage counselor say, "You cannot work on your relationship; you can only work on yourself." If the husband or wife does change, it will be because he or she has willingly done so.

When I was a freshman in college, I had a 7:30 a.m. class on Monday, Wednesday, and Friday. A college boy, I had the freedom to do whatever I wanted on Sunday night, Tuesday night, and Thursday night. Midnight pizza runs with my buddies? No problem. There were no parents around to question the wisdom of such a thing. But after a few weeks of being sleep-deprived and feeling sick to my stomach in that class, I decided to stop the silliness. No one made me cut back on late nights before my early-morning class. *I* made me cut back. The misery of not doing this wasn't worth the pepperoni and extra cheese. I made the change because I wanted to make the change. I saw something better and chose it.

YOUR ROLE AND YOUR JOB DESCRIPTION AS YOUR WIFE'S SHEPHERD ARE BETWEEN GOD AND YOU.

This book is intended to encourage you to be a gentle shepherd, to love your wife as she has never been loved before, to serve her confidently and "give your life" to her. Like the sun in Aesop's fable, you may win her heart by warming her. And you will gain no ground by force. Think shepherd, not cowboy.

You're Doing It Wrong, Jack

Whatever your wife's disposition, you should never—*never*—remind her that you're the shepherd. You should never need to. You should never tell her about the shepherd's rod and staff. You should never need to.

You should be so adept at fulfilling this role that you never need to mention it. Your role and your job description as your wife's shepherd are between God and you. Your wife doesn't need to know anything about the strategy. But don't worry—based on the way you are treating her, she'll be able to tell.

If you'll forgive me, I'm reminded of Jack Butler (Michael Keaton) in the movie *Mr. Mom*. He has just dropped his kids off in front of

THE REALITY OF A SHEPHERD PROVIDING EXACTLY WHAT YOUR WIFE NEEDS SHOULD BE JUST LIKE THAT. YOUR PROMISE TO COMFORT HER WILL BRING YOUR WIFE A SENSE OF CONFIDENCE. AND WHOLENESS. AND JOY.

their school, but because he's new to carpooling, he's going north and the line of cars is going south. Annette, the mom in charge, holds her hand up and Jack stops his car. He rolls down his window and the sheriff speaks.

Annette: "Hello, Jack, I'm Annette."
Jack: "Hello, Annette."
Annette: "You're doing it wrong."

If you find yourself needing to tell your wife that you're her shepherd or if you feel the need to tell her that you're the leader in your marriage or, perish the thought, if you ask her to "submit" to you, my friend, you're doing it wrong.

"I will set shepherds over them who will care for them, and they shall fear no more, nor be dismayed, neither shall any be missing, declares the LORD." (Jeremiah 23:4)

Telling your wife about your role as her shepherd should be like describing to a fish the makeup of water. The only thing a fish knows about water is that it provides a safe environment for him to live and flourish. She feels so safe there she doesn't need to think about it. Or question it.

The reality of a shepherd providing exactly what your wife needs should be just like that. Your promise to comfort her will bring your wife a sense of confidence. And wholeness. And joy.

ELEVEN

A SHEPHERD FEEDS HIS SHEEP

You prepare a table before me in the presence of my enemies....

—PSALM 23:5

The first time I walked into Nancy Leigh DeMoss's kitchen, I noticed something conspicuously odd. Nancy—in her fifties and never married—had no children or grandchildren, but there in her kitchen, almost obstructing the passage from the dining area to the outdoor deck, was a highchair. This contraption, its big plastic tray a launching pad from which toddlers lob their Cheerios, is well known to every parent, but what was it doing in Nancy's kitchen?

And then something dawned on me that further endeared this woman to me. Nancy was so faithful in hosting families, even families with small children, that a highchair was a permanent fixture. It was a symbol of what was important to her. And as I met her friends, I discovered that some had not only visited but had actually lived in her house—for weeks, months, even years. Although Nancy appreciates cleanliness and order, they matter less to her than making visiting families feel at home. Feeding friends. What a good thing.

Preparing a Table

When the Psalmist wrote that the Good Shepherd prepares a table for him, he meant that the Lord is a good host. If we're going to take our shepherding cues from the Lord, this is something we must seriously consider.

Like Nancy, Bobbie was serious about hospitality. We lived in a small neighborhood in Orlando for sixteen years. During those years we probably hosted fifty parties. And if you were to ask those neighbors, they would tell you that our house represented hospitality of the highest order. Bobbie did that.

"What if I'm not a cook?" you could rightly ask. "Not only that, but sometimes my wife shoos me out of the kitchen when she's getting ready for company." Ah yes, been there, heard that. So when you and your wife are hosting friends, what else could you do to help?

I know a husband who is useless as a cook but claims to be a world-class chair-mover, table-setter, and kitchen-cleaner-upper. He's also good at expressing gratitude to his wife for being such an amazing hostess. This guy can do these things without troubling his wife as she prepares for a dinner party. Before guests arrive, he walks through the house to make sure things are picked up and in order. He

> WE THOUGHT WE WERE DOING THE DISHES, BUT WE WERE DOING WHAT FAMILIES HAVE BEEN DOING FOR CENTURIES— WORKING TOGETHER, LAUGHING TOGETHER, AND LEARNING TO LOVE EACH OTHER IN THE PROCESS. AND ALL THIS HAPPENED IN THE KITCHEN.

completes these tasks without being asked and without drawing attention to himself. This guy also shares the responsibility of welcoming guests as they arrive and stands at the door as they leave to thank them for coming.

"This guy" for president.

Ask your wife if you have anything to learn from this guy's playbook. If she says yes, go for it. You won't need to turn in your man card. I promise.

You're the Shepherd of the Center of Your Home

In a contemporary context, "preparing a table before me" is primarily about the kitchen. My parents didn't get a dishwasher until I was in college, so we usually did the dishes after dinner together as a family. I would stand next to my mother, drying the dishes she had just washed and rinsed, snapping the dishtowel at my siblings when she wasn't looking.

We thought we were doing the dishes, but we were doing what families have been doing for centuries—working together, laughing together, and learning to love each other in the process. And all this happened in the kitchen.

The room where your kitchen table sits is the center of your home. As nice as it might be to have extra rooms and technological niceties, you cannot afford to let your children check in and out like hotel patrons. On a regular basis, you must draw them back to the kitchen table.

And I really did mean to say that *you* must draw them back to the kitchen. You are the shepherd of the kitchen table, even if you're not the chef. The responsibility for what happens at mealtime is yours. It's part of your commission.

"But," you might argue, "our family's schedule is crazy. Soccer practice, play rehearsals, gymnastics, and piano lessons on top of school and church activities make sitting down together for a meal almost impossible." No doubt. So let's be reasonable and insist on only *one* family meal a day. No one knows more about mealtime than the Italians, so listen to the renowned Italian cookbook author Marcella Hazan: "I'm saddened because there isn't much that brings families together these days. But we all have to eat to stay alive, so why not...enjoy [meals] as a family? It worries me that in America family mealtime is falling by the wayside because people believe they are too busy."[1] She's right. Even though our schedules are filled with activities, we're *not* too busy for this. And if we are, then something besides family mealtime needs to go.

One more thing: *no cellphones at the table.* Family dinners that count cannot include a cellphone in everyone's hands or lap. They're not welcome guests. At this writing, I have five grandchildren, ages fifteen to twenty-one. I have had multiple mealtimes at their parents' homes. Their dads—my sons-in-law—are not domestic tyrants. They are kind, reasonable, and fair. But, as the shepherds of their kitchens, they have made a rule for the whole family. No cellphones. And they and their wives follow this rule too.

> *NO CELLPHONES AT THE TABLE.* **FAMILY DINNERS THAT COUNT CANNOT INCLUDE A CELLPHONE IN EVERYONE'S HANDS OR LAP. THEY'RE NOT WELCOME GUESTS.**

Mealtime with God . . . in the Presence of My Enemies

When King David wrote, "You prepare a table," he was, of course, saying that the God of the universe is the host of this meal.

About mealtime with our Good Shepherd, Charles Spurgeon said, "Nothing is hurried, there is no confusion, no disturbance, the enemy is at the door, and yet God prepares a table, and the Christian sits down and eats as if everything were in perfect peace."[2] Whether you're newly married, or your house is crawling with little ones, or you're empty-nesters, take a minute and read that again. Insert the word "couple" or "family" after the word "Christian." Take a deep breath and read it again.

YOU CAN CALL ANY DISTRACTIONS TO A PEACEFUL MEAL WITH YOUR FAMILY ENEMIES. BECAUSE THEY ARE.

The last thing Jesus did before His trial and crucifixion was to have a quiet meal with His closest friends. His enemies—cynics, skeptics, critics, Satan himself—were lurking just outside the door, but for now, the "table was set." Jesus was there with His friends. You can call any distractions to a peaceful meal with your family enemies. Because they are.

Hunger Loves Company

The God Who created us could have given us perpetually self-sustaining bodies. But He didn't. Instead, we were designed to get hungry. Every four hours or so, having completely digested our last meal, we get hungry again. And often this appetite for more food inspires us to call a meeting. "Let's get together for lunch," we will say to a friend with whom we're eager to catch up. Or "Nancy and I would love to have your family over for dinner."

How fascinating—how wonderful—that several times a day we crave food, and more often than not, we satisfy this craving with friends and family.

Dinner at the DeMoss Home

The highchair at Nancy's house and her gift of hospitality were passed down from her parents. Art and Nancy DeMoss (her mother is named Nancy, too) were so convinced of the sacred power of mealtimes that they hosted *thousands* of guests at their home in Philadelphia in the 1970s. In addition to honoring these guests with an elegant meal, the other purpose of these dinners was to tell them about how they could receive salvation through the love, mercy, and forgiveness of Jesus.

A successful businessman who had converted to Christ in his twenties, Art DeMoss determined that he and his wife could do nothing more important than "set a table before" people who didn't know the Good Shepherd. And these dinners were legendary.

When he died suddenly on the tennis court in 1979 at the age of fifty-three, Art DeMoss had been influential in leading tens of thousands of people to Christ. Many of these people had come to the dinners and, through the DeMoss' hospitality and bold witness, had come to know Jesus as their Savior. If ever a family defined the word "legacy," this is it.

The Marriage Supper

When I proposed marriage to Nancy in May 2015 and she said "yes, with all my heart," we began talking about our wedding. The way we saw it, we had two choices. We could elope to some deserted island or we could host a big wedding. The second choice prevailed. At our stage of life, we both had a sweet and large collection of family and friends, and we wanted to "showcase the loveliness of Christ." We were also eager to point our guests to our Good Shepherd, the One the Bible calls our Bridegroom. The people who believe in Him— the church—are called His bride. Following the ceremony we all had a meal. Together.

This meal, which we call our "Marriage Supper," is not original with us. In his vision of the end of time, the Apostle John records, "And the angel said to me, 'Write this: Blessed are those who are invited to the marriage supper of the Lamb.'" (Revelation 19:9) This will be the ultimate mealtime, shared with millions who, down through history, have committed their lives in faith to Christ.

WE SIT NEXT TO A BROTHER AND ACROSS FROM A SISTER. AND AT THIS TABLE, NO ONE IS DISTRACTED...OR TEMPTED TO GLANCE AT HIS SMARTPHONE.

You and I are in good company. Jesus is also the "Shepherd of the kitchen." He welcomes us and invites His own to the table and gathers us around it. We feast on His goodness, His mercy, and His grace. We sit next to a brother and across from a sister. And at this table, no one is distracted...or tempted to glance at his smartphone.

When the Good Shepherd Is Upset

Called to be shepherds with the Lord as our model, we find ourselves in an imperfect, sinful world. Stuff happens. Things break. We break. We get caught in traffic when we're already late to a meeting, ordinarily reliable colleagues let us down, we let ourselves down, and anger—maybe rage—erupts.

Years ago, I was teaching my Sunday school class from the Apostle Paul's letter to the Ephesians. Bible scholars agree that the central message of this letter is summarized in the first two verses of chapter 5: "Therefore be imitators of God, as beloved children. And walk in love, as Christ loved us and gave himself up for us, a fragrant offering and sacrifice to God." This sounds a lot like what we're talking about, doesn't it? Paul could have written, "Walk in love and live *like the Shepherd*."

One day, as I was preparing the next Sunday's lesson, this verse jumped off the page: "Be angry but do not sin; do not let the sun go down on your anger, and give no opportunity to the devil." (Ephesians 4:26) I wondered, does God get angry, and if so what does He get angry about? It seemed to me that we have permission to get angry at the things that make God angry. Fair enough? Yes.

But, before teaching that class, I had to make a business trip to Dallas. As soon as I had sat down on the plane and fastened my seatbelt, a young man in the next seat greeted me, and we started a conversation. He learned that I was a writer and a teacher, and I soon learned that he was in love with a "beautiful woman." In fact, he was headed to Dallas to inform her parents that he was moving in with her.

The young man watched my face as he told me he and his girlfriend were in love and had decided that living together seemed like "the right thing to do." I watched him as he watched me. A pregnant pause, and then with my pulse quickening, I said, "This is a problem."

A PREGNANT PAUSE, AND THEN WITH MY PULSE QUICKENING, I SAID, "THIS IS A PROBLEM."

Stunned by what I had just said, he blanched, and his eyes widened. We talked nonstop until the wheels screeched our welcome to DFW. I liked this guy. And although I was not going to be able to talk him out of this decision, he seemed receptive to what I was saying. He even let me say a short prayer with him as the plane taxied to the gate. I prayed that the Lord would speak to him.

Later, as I went over the conversation in my mind, I kept thinking, "A man and woman take their marriage out for a test drive. This makes God angry."

On my return flight from Dallas to Orlando, my seatmate was a woman.

Pretty and articulate, she looked to be in her early twenties. She went first with the questions. After the opening "Where are you headed?" and "What do you do for a living?" it was my turn. She had just finished graduate school and was starting her career with a large corporation in central Florida. Her boyfriend lived just outside of Orlando. They had met on a blind date a few months before, and she was headed to see him. Well actually, she was headed to Florida to move in with him.

> LIKE A GOOD SHEPHERD WHO CARES DEEPLY FOR US, GOD GETS ANGRY AT SIN. WHY? BECAUSE HE KNOWS THAT, LIKE A CANCER, SIN RUINS HIS FLOCK. SIN CRUSHES HIS SHEEP.

"Seriously?" I thought to myself. "What's going on here? Clearly déjà vu."

I let her finish telling me how wonderful this guy was. And then she stopped talking. It seemed like she was eager to hear what I had to say about what she had to say. So in a replay of my conversation with the young man on the flight to Dallas, I gently said, "This is a problem."

Early Sunday morning, as I put the finishing touches on my lesson, the answer to my hypothetical question the week before—What makes God angry?—came into sharp focus. Like a Good Shepherd who cares deeply for us, God gets angry at sin. Why? Because He knows that, like a cancer, sin ruins His flock. Sin crushes His sheep.

You and I have God's permission to be upset. Angry. When people choose to act in ways that will ultimately hurt them, crush them, destroy them, our Good Shepherd gets ticked off. Not for His sake. For ours.

RSVP

Several years later I found something else about God's anger in a familiar Gospel story that I had never noticed before. It's in Jesus' parable of a great supper:

A man once gave a great banquet and invited many. And at the time for the banquet he sent his servant to say to those who had been invited, "Come, for everything is now ready." But they all alike began to make excuses. The first said to him, "I have bought a field, and I must go out and see it. Please have me excused." And another said, "I have bought five yoke of oxen, and I go to examine them. Please have me excused." And another said, "I have married a wife, and therefore I cannot come." So the servant came and reported these things to his master. (Luke 14:16–21)

In this parable, the master—the Good Shepherd—is Christ, and His invitation has been extended to a world of sheep. But the invited friends all decline. After all, they're busy people. They appreciate the invitation and they'd *like* to come, they really would. But the busyness of life has closed in on them, and they just can't make it.

Now here's what I noticed for the first time. In this parable, Jesus says something that He rarely says in the Gospels: "Then the master of the house became angry.... " (Luke 14:21) How interesting. We're not surprised if God's wrath is kindled when He sees His people destroyed by the ravages of sin, when disobedience to His precepts impales their souls. But not coming to a dinner? This makes Him angry? Really? Yes. I guess it does. But why? Let me, if I may, take a run at the answer to this question.

TO TURN DOWN THE SHEPHERD'S INVITATION TO DINNER IS TO TURN DOWN HIS OFFER OF GRACE AND MERCY.

When King David wrote, "You prepare a table before me in the presence of my enemies," he wasn't describing a spontaneous "Ya'll come over for a little something to eat" affair. This meal was planned before the universe was spoken into existence. Coming to the Shepherd's table is a matter of life and death. We ignore the invitation at our own peril.

To turn down the Shepherd's invitation to dinner is to turn down His offer of grace and mercy. His life and death secured these for us. Saying no to this dinner invitation is not just a clumsy social *faux pas*. It's denying life-giving oxygen when we're dead as a stone at the bottom of the sea.

Meal Times Should Be Protected

Christians should follow the lead of our Jewish friends and treat family mealtime as sacred. The prayers that fathers have prayed at the Passover meal for millennia include this passage:

> Blessed are You, Lord, our G-d,[3] King of the universe, benevolent G-d, our Father, our King, our Might, our Creator, our Redeemer, our Maker, our Holy One, the Holy One of Jacob, our Shepherd, the Shepherd of Israel, the King who is good and does good to all, each and every day. He has done good for us, He does good for us, and He will do good for us; He has bestowed, He bestows, and He will forever bestow upon us grace, kindness, and mercy, relief, salvation and success, blessing and help, consolation, sustenance and nourishment, compassion, life, peace, and all goodness; and may He never cause us to lack any good.

Soon after Nancy and I began dating, we learned that we had something precious in common. From the time we were both small, our dads "held court" at dinnertime. Of course, neither Art DeMoss nor Sam Wolgemuth was heavy-handed about this tradition, but both of these men knew the value of having all their children, knees under the same table, eating, talking, and enjoying each other.

WHEN WE SIT AT THE TABLE OF OUR GOOD SHEPHERD AND WHEN WE SIT AS GODLY SHEPHERDS AT OUR OWN FAMILY TABLE, WE ARE KEEPING OUR ENEMIES AT BAY.

As best they could, they made family dinners a high priority. As a newly married young man in 1970, I brought this tradition into my home. Even though it was just Bobbie and me, grabbing all our meals on the run felt wrong, even sacrilegious. When our children came along, we kept the tradition alive, and now the custom continues in their homes. They and their husbands and their families will tell you how special—sacred— these times are.

A Quick Revisit to Those Enemies

The author of Psalm 23 was a shepherd, a warrior, and a king, so his enemies must have been diverse—and legion. When we sit at the table of our Good Shepherd and when we sit as godly shepherds at our own family table, we are keeping our enemies at bay. We are not succumbing to their wiles and schemes. Our enemies like David's, whisper in our ears. "Hey, you're busy. You don't need to sit down with your wife and kids. Just grab something on the run. Again. They'll understand."

You and I are the shepherds of our kitchens and our mealtimes, our wives and our flock. We must not shirk this privilege.

We are leading humbly. We are leading faithfully. We are leading well.

Hold Fast . . . Don't Let Go

I might be accused of making too much of mealtimes. I don't mind. I'll take the criticism in stride. I'm good with the "slings and arrows." Because this is truth. It is right.

Our Good Shepherd prepares a table for us with Him. And we do the same with our wives and families.

A Post Script about Food

Although we've talked primarily about mealtimes and food in this chapter, there is more to food than meets the palate. "The Lord himself is my inheritance, my prize. He is my food and drink, my highest joy! He guards all that is mine." (Psalm 16:5 TLB)

Our job as the shepherd is to include God in the dinnertime conversation. Of course, every meal should start with thanking your Heavenly Father for His provision. Other ways to include God could be as intentional as reading from the Bible or a devotional book. Or it could be a spontaneous "Isn't God amazing?" moment because of something extraordinary that happened that day.

King David referred to the Good Shepherd as "inheritance, my prize, my highest joy." Who wouldn't want this on the menu?

TWELVE

A SHEPHERD ENCOURAGES HIS SHEEP

You anoint my head with oil....
—PSALM 23:5

Instruction does much, but encouragement everything.
—JOHANN WOLFGANG VON GOETHE

There's an expression in football, "blocking and tackling." You have probably heard it even if you never played. You may have used this expression yourself.

The glamour assignments in football involve running with the ball and throwing and receiving passes. Success in these positions puts you in the headlines and garners eye-popping paychecks. Prowess in blocking and tackling, on the other hand, may get you a swat on the backside and an "attaboy" from the coach after the game, an expression of appreciation to savor as you nurse sore muscles and bite wounds on your forearms.

Your primary job as a member of the "front line" is to protect the showoffs who are passing and running. You're responsible for the basics. The fundamentals. Blocking and tackling. Now don't worry. Even though you may think that we have just left our shepherd guy standing in his bathrobe out in the field, we're not leaving the big idea of shepherding. You'll see what I mean in a minute.

Your Three Amigos

In May 2005, my alma mater, Taylor University, awarded me an honorary doctorate, a recognition that comes with the privilege of addressing the audience at the graduation ceremonies. My challenge to the graduates that sunny afternoon in the football stadium—see the connection now with football?—was pretty fundamental. Blocking and tackling, you might say. Not much glamour, but mightily important.

"Now that you're leaving college and headed out on your own," I said, "you need to start looking for three different people to be a part of your life. You need a 'Paul,' a 'Timothy,' and a 'Barnabas.'" Everyone needs someone in his life who teaches and instructs. Looking at the assembled Taylor faculty, I thanked them for being Pauls in their students' lives. Turning to the students, I said, "But now that you're graduating, you're going to need to replace at least one of these people, the Paul in your life."

Continuing, I told them, "Second, you need a Timothy, someone into whom you have the opportunity to pour your life." If they led a Bible study on campus or had a chance to mentor a younger student, they had their Timothy. But now that they were leaving town, they would need to find someone else.

Finally, everyone needs a Barnabas. "Look around you," I suggested. "Which of your classmates has been a Barnabas to you, an encourager? Who has picked you up when you have fallen? Who gives you a fresh dose of kindness and grace each day? Maybe you're headed to your wedding. This seems to happen to a lot of seniors." Some laughter rose from under the mortarboards, and I thought to myself, "If you are, I sure hope you're marrying your encourager, your Barnabas."

Graduating seniors aren't the only ones who need a Paul, a Timothy, and a Barnabas in their life. We all do, especially those of us called to be shepherds.

Paul

We know quite a lot about the life of Saul of Tarsus, a tent-maker and Pharisee who, with a new name and a new passion, became the Apostle of the Gentiles. Much of the New Testament was written by or about him. A well-educated and zealous Jew, he hated the new sect devoted to Jesus of Nazareth and persecuted its followers. Then, on the road to Damascus, a huge flash of light knocked Saul off his horse. Seeing Jesus and hearing His voice, Saul experienced the most famous conversion in history, tenaciously following his new Lord for the rest of his life.

Paul, as he became known, was a road warrior. He helped to found and build churches throughout Asia Minor, eventually bringing his ministry to Rome, where he was brutally martyred for the sake of Christ.

As you read the Acts of the Apostles and Paul's letters, you come across name after name of men and women Paul mentored, and of course there must have been countless others whose names were not recorded. What stories each of these people could tell about being led to Christ by Paul. If you think you're busy, imagine being responsible for Paul's to-do list, yet he found the time to teach and guide and form each person individually, building the first generation of the church.

You and I need a Paul.

Timothy

Another way of introducing this important man named Timothy is to say that he was one of the guys who had a Paul in his life. As a matter of fact, Timothy had *the* Paul in his life. Timothy was one of Paul's protégés. He was an understudy, a disciple of Paul. Everyone needs a Timothy in his life, someone into whose mind and heart and life he can pour truth, guided and shaped by experience, victories, and failure.

THE GREAT BENEFIT OF BEING THE TEACHER IS THAT YOU LEARN FAR MORE THAN THE STUDENTS EVER WILL.

I have had the privilege of teaching Sunday school since 1969. An amateur—a layman—I stand with my Bible open in front of me and do my best to help others understand what the Scriptures have to say. As you know, the great benefit of being the teacher is that you learn far more than the students ever will. The people who have sat through my lessons—my Timothys—have been necessary for me to get serious about studying God's Word. And the Lord has granted me the privilege of meeting some of the Timothys one on one, for breakfast or lunch. Each of these men has been a gift to me.

The Timothy in your life may need you as his master craftsman; but in many ways you need him even more than he needs you.

Barnabas

One of the earliest followers of the Apostles was a man called Joseph. He must have played an important role in the infant church, because they gave him the nickname Barnabas, meaning "son of encouragement" (Acts 4:36). This takes me back to those eager graduating seniors. If I could have lifted my voice to "televangelist levels," I would have implored them, "If you are losing your 'encouragement friend,' find a Barnabas—fast!"

In chapter three I told the story about my moving to Michigan from Florida. A sixty-seven-year-old widower, I did this because I was in love with Nancy and didn't want her to uproot her life, even though she would have done so cheerfully. I knew that I was called to make this move. I left a Paul and a few Timothys behind in central Florida, and there were plenty of Barnabases back there as well. But I moved because I was about to marry a Barnabas. My own Barnabas. A woman of encouragement.

And I knew exactly what it was like to be married to a Barnabas.

I've Lost My Coach, My Cheerleader

In the weeks that followed Bobbie's death in 2014, I spent many evenings by myself in the darkness of my living room. I sat on the green couch, across the corner from the red chair that was Bobbie's. She sat there to read her Bible, to pray, and to journal tens of thousands of words. It was the chair where she was perched when I kneeled next to her during the final months of her life before the men from hospice wrestled a large hospital bed into our house.

In those first few weeks, the grief and loss hung like an ominous and dark cloud on a Florida spring day. Then, late one night, a thought blasted into my consciousness so forcefully that I said it aloud: "I've lost my coach, my cheerleader." And a line from a Joni Mitchell song stole into my head, "Don't it always seem to go / That you don't know what you've got till it's gone."

I had always tried to appreciate what I had in my marriage to a remarkable woman, but in the thick blackness of that night, I realized that I had often taken Bobbie's encouragement for granted. I didn't truly appreciate what I had, and now it was gone.

O My Man, I Love Him So

Sometimes, over the forty-four years of our marriage, when I stepped into the kitchen, briefcase in hand, after a long day at the office, Bobbie would greet me with a song from *Funny Girl*, draping her arms around my neck as she sang,

> Oh, my man, I love him so,
> He'll never know
> All my life was just despair
> Until he was there.[1]

And how did this woman take on the role of my encourager? I went first. And how did I know what this encouragement looked like? My mother taught me.

When my dad came home from work, my mother would set down whatever she was doing and greet him at the back door. She did not sing her greeting, although she did have a lovely voice. She welcomed her husband home with a hug and a kiss and "It's so good to see you, Samuel. How was your day? I love you."

Grace Wolgemuth was a Barnabas to my dad. She encouraged him. Her expressions of love and her words of kindness made him the man the world knew and loved. The leader of an international youth ministry, my dad would speak to audiences of thousands, often inviting my mother to stand next to him as he introduced her. He called her "Grace by my side." I'll say she was.

My mother was also an encourager to me. As I was growing up, my dad instructed me in what it means to follow Christ, modeling integrity and solid character. But my mother spent my childhood in the grandstands, cheering her son on. It was as though

MY MOTHER SPENT MY CHILDHOOD IN THE GRANDSTANDS, CHEERING HER SON ON.

she was shouting, "Come on, Robert, I'm pulling for you! You can do it." And sometimes I did.

Because I saw Barnabas modeled so well and knew that Bobbie had not seen much of this as a young woman, I decided to go first.

On the Front Row, Cheering

In 1975, soon after our second daughter was born, Bobbie was offered a chance to become a "gospel singing star." She had as clear, strong, and compelling a voice as other women who were making it big in Christian music, and she had the stage presence to match. A demo tape and a conversation with a producer let us both know that she would be rewarded handsomely if she'd take this step.

"What should I do?" she asked me late one night. In the living room of our little house in Glenview, Illinois, we knelt and prayed. The next morning we talked.

"You have an amazing voice," I said to her over breakfast. "And if the Lord calls you to do this, I'll do everything I can to encourage you and help make it possible." As Bobbie's cheerleader—and given the example and witness of my own mother—I went first. As you might imagine, having received my encouragement, she became an encourager herself, and her lavish encouragement became the single most meaningful gift she gave me.

The Barnabas Gene: Nancy's Encouragement Heritage

Today I'm married to a woman who also understands the power of an encouraging word, given and received. Nancy receives emails, notes, and words of kindness and support from around the world. And, she goes first—I've carried stacks of encouraging handwritten notes from Nancy to the mailbox many times—and people often reciprocate.

As it turns out, Nancy inherited this skill from her mother who was a Barnabas to *her* shepherd, her husband. You don't need to take my word for it, because we have a letter that Art DeMoss's wife wrote to one of his new employees. It reads:

> Though I don't talk about this in public for obvious reasons, I am married to a truly unique man—one who is both godly and a genius, totally committed to doing God's will (at any cost), absolutely trustworthy, very transparent (it's never necessary to read "between the lines"), a devoted father and husband (also an exciting one!), someone who encourages growth in all of us (as he's constantly challenging himself to mental and spiritual growth), a loyal friend and one so full of love that at times it's not possible to receive it all!
>
> Having said all this, it appears that Art is perfect. Of course, that's not true, as we both know. However, I sincerely believe that the only reason God has entrusted so much talent and treasure to Art is that the Lord knew he could be trusted.
>
> Even though he *is* all that I described (and much more!), he's also extremely humble.
>
> I guess that makes me sound naïve or unrealistic, or just terribly prejudiced. But after twenty-one years of living

with this man, I truly believe I am the most uniquely blessed woman in the world.

Two weeks after that letter was written, Art DeMoss died of a heart attack. Whether or not he ever knew about that particular letter, it reflects a deep admiration that had to have touched every aspect of their marriage.

When Nancy shared that letter of her mother's with me, she wrote, "Robert, as we continue to pray and discern God's will for our marriage and our future, I want to be to you all He has made me to be—as a wife, friend, encourager, partner, and lover." Sewn to Nancy's DNA is a Barnabas gene. Her mother encouraged her husband. Nancy inherited this gift and now I'm the grateful recipient.

> **SEWN TO NANCY'S DNA IS A BARNABAS GENE. HER MOTHER ENCOURAGED HER HUSBAND. NANCY INHERITED THIS GIFT AND NOW I'M THE GRATEFUL RECIPIENT.**

Here's an important secret. A husband has the privilege of going first, of being a Barnabas to his wife. His encouragement fills her heart. Whatever else her shepherd provides for her, she knows that he will be an encourager. Ask your wife if your encouragement means anything to her. She'll tell you.

You Anoint My Head with Oil: Encouraged to a Special Task

Shepherds protect their flocks from the sun, from deadly parasites, and from snakes and vermin by pouring oil on their heads and working it into their wool. In the Old Testament we see how this practical ritual took on deep significance among the Chosen People.

Instructing Moses about the consecration of Aaron, the first priest of the covenant, God told him, "And you shall take the anointing oil, and pour it on his head and anoint him." (Exodus 29:7) The

You are your wife's earthly priest. God has given you the authority to anoint your wife symbolically with your encouragement and words of blessing.

kings of Israel were also anointed with oil, beginning with Saul (1 Samuel 10:1). When the shepherd boy David was presented to the prophet Samuel, "the LORD said, 'Arise, anoint him; for this is he.' Then Samuel took the horn of oil, and anointed him in the midst of his brothers; and the Spirit of the LORD came mightily upon David from that day forward." (1 Samuel 16:12–13)

Throughout the Scriptures, when God called someone to a special task, His priest or prophet anointed him with oil, a symbol of his vocation.

You are your wife's earthly priest. God has given you the authority to anoint your wife symbolically with your encouragement and words of blessing. You hold her and pray for her. And you don't have to ask permission to do this, "For the husband is the head of the wife even as Christ is the head of the church, his body, and is himself its Savior." (Ephesians 5:23)

The implications of this are astonishing. God has given you the responsibility and the privilege to be the spiritual leader—the priest—of your marriage.

No Search Committee Necessary

I once served as the chairman of my church's pastor nominating committee as we searched nationwide for a new senior minister. Sorting through all those résumés was an arduous task. But there's no need for a committee to find just the right spiritual leader for your home. Why? Because *you* are that leader. God has given you the responsibility of being your family's priest just like Job, a family priest in the Old Testament we sometimes overlook.

"And when the days of the feast had run their course, Job would send and consecrate them, and he would rise early in the morning and offer burnt offerings according to the number of them all. For Job said, 'It may be that my children have sinned, and cursed God in their hearts.' Thus Job did continually." (Job 1:5)

Although the book of Job appears in your Bible after the historical books, most scholars believe that it was written during an earlier period, before priests from the Jewish family of Levi were assigned the duty of leading God's people in worship. So Job, a "blameless...man of complete integrity" (1:1), had the responsibility of being the "priest" for his wife and family. Before there were professionals to fulfill this duty, there was the family's father.

In addition to Job, there was the great boat-building "preacher of righteousness" (2 Peter 2:5). He's one of my favorite Bible characters.

Then Noah built an altar to the LORD and took some of every clean bird and offered burnt offerings on the altar. And when the LORD smelled the pleasing aroma, the LORD said in his heart, "I will never again curse the ground because of man, for the intentions of man's heart is evil from his youth." (Genesis 8:20–21)

> **NOAH PROBABLY BROUGHT HIS WIFE AND HIS FAMILY TO THE ALTAR FOR THE PURPOSE OF REPENTANCE AND WORSHIP.**

Noah was his family's priest—an ordinary husband and father with an extraordinary love for God and an obedient heart. "Noah was a just man, perfect in his generation. Noah walked with God" (Genesis 6:9). Like Job, Noah probably brought his wife and his family to the altar for the purpose of repentance and worship.

For centuries, until Moses received the Ten Commandments on Mount Sinai after God delivered the Israelites from Egypt, fathers took the role as the priests in their homes. In fact, the first Passover celebration that saved the children of Israel from the tenth plague—the death of the firstborn—was performed *in every single home*. It was as though ordinary Jewish homes become house churches.

In the Old Testament, God is our Good Shepherd. In the New Testament, Jesus Christ, God's perfect Son, came to earth as our Shepherd-Priest.

"Seeing then that we have a great High Priest who has passed through the heavens, Jesus the Son of God, let us hold fast our confession. For we do not have a High Priest who cannot sympathize with our weaknesses, but was in all points tempted as we are, yet without sin. Let us therefore come boldly to the throne of grace that we may obtain mercy and find grace to help in time of need." (Hebrews 4:14–16)

The Apostle Peter explains that we participate in Christ's priesthood: "But you are a chosen race, a royal priesthood, a holy nation, a people for his own possession." (1 Peter 2:9) Peter wasn't lecturing in a seminary when he wrote these words; he was speaking to ordinary folks like you and me.

You Anoint My Head with Oil: The Holy Spirit's Presence

Fulfilling His call as our Good Shepherd, Jesus pours anointing oil on you and me, His sheep. When we trust Him as our Savior—our Shepherd—He fills us with His Holy Spirit and commissions us. "But you have an anointing from the Holy One, and you know all things." (1 John 2:20) As our wife's earthly shepherd, we have the joy of leading her to the same anointing experience with her Good Shepherd. What greater encouragement could she find than the presence of God?

Soon after Bobbie and I were married in 1970, someone encouraged us to pray together every night before going to sleep. In this prayer, I would encourage my wife and pronounce a blessing on her, inviting our Shepherd to hover over our rest that night. Bobbie rarely missed the chance to thank me for taking the time to do this.

Now Nancy loves when I pray with her at night and always thanks me. Then, before we doze off, she softly whispers, "May the Lord bless your sleep."

Each night, I have the privilege—and the shepherd's responsibility—to anoint my wife with the protective oil of the Holy Spirit by way of prayer. This invites the Lord to be present and is an encouragement to her. It is my duty to do this. It is my honor.

> NANCY LOVES WHEN I PRAY WITH HER AT NIGHT AND ALWAYS THANKS ME. THEN, BEFORE WE DOZE OFF, SHE SOFTLY WHISPERS, "MAY THE LORD BLESS YOUR SLEEP."

A Tall Order for You?

The idea of praying together may seem strange to you. Maybe you never saw your parents do such a thing, so you have no model to follow. Or maybe you don't like the idea of praying in public—even if your wife is your only "audience." This has not been a struggle for me because I heard my dad pray publicly many times—something for which I'm grateful—but I do know how challenging this can be for some men. Maybe you.

After the Sunday morning collection at the large church I attended in Nashville, four deacons would walk down the center aisle and present the tithes and offerings at the front of the church, where one of them would pray a blessing. The service was broadcast live throughout Middle Tennessee, so the deacon's prayer was heard by thousands of worshippers. He usually had a week's notice, and more often than not he had his prayer written out on a piece of paper on top of the offering plates.

One Sunday I was among this quartet of ushers. As we were about to process down the center aisle with the "baskets of bounty," one of the deacons whispered to another, "You have the prayer this morning, right?" The poor man's eyes widened, and his face lost all color. When the jokester realized that his prank had had more than the intended effect, he pulled the written prayer out of his pocket and with a wink laid it on top of his own offering plate. "No problem," he whispered. "I have it." Funny now; not funny then.

BUDDIES ARE A GOOD IDEA. THEY CAN MEAN SAFETY.

Praying out loud may not come naturally for you—even just one shepherd and his sheep. That's okay. There are tools to help you. When a couple who were new believers told Nancy and me about their strong apprehension about praying together, we bought two copies of *Two Hearts Praying as One* by Dennis and Barbara Rainey, one for us and one for them. For the next month or so, the four of us read this book together—they in Florida and we in Michigan. Even for veterans, this little book provided a lovely and easy-to-follow template for praying together.

You Anoint My Head with Oil: Healing

If you went to summer camp as a youngster, you may remember the "buddy system," which is especially important if there's a lake on the campground. Many years ago, when I was in youth work, I was visiting possible venues for a high school summer camp. At one camp, the water was frothing with young boys. Loud peals of laughter and joy rang through the large trees surrounding the lake. Then one of the lifeguards perched on a tall stand, blew his whistle and shouted through a bullhorn: "Buddies! Buddies! Buddies!"

Instantly each of the boys began searching for his pre-assigned buddy. And when they found each other, like the referee with the hand of the winner at the end of a boxing match, they stood still, their hands clasped in the air. When every boy had found his buddy, and the water had stilled, the lifeguard blew his whistle again and the chaos resumed.

Buddies are a good idea. They can mean safety.

One of my favorite passages in the Gospels is found in the sixth chapter of Mark. The disciples have gone through healings and rejection and crowd control—all in a day's work when you're traveling with the Messiah. Then Jesus calls his twelve together for a strategy meeting and sends them out "two by two" (6:7)—the buddy system. Mark records the results of the disciples' missionary foray a few verses later: "And they cast out many demons, and anointed with oil many who were sick and healed them." (6:13)

Your wife may not be crazy about a nickname like "Buddy," but this is what she is to you. You are the shepherd and she is your sheep—your companion, your friend. You verbally bless her with the reminder of the lavish oil of God's Holy Spirit and her soul is healed.

> YOUR WIFE MAY NOT BE CRAZY ABOUT A NICKNAME LIKE "BUDDY," BUT THIS IS WHAT SHE IS TO YOU. YOU ARE THE SHEPHERD AND SHE IS YOUR SHEEP—YOUR COMPANION, YOUR FRIEND.

The Power of Two

There have been many memorable pairs in musical history—Mozart and Da Ponte, Gilbert and Sullivan, Rodgers and Hammerstein—but none was more successful than John Lennon and Paul McCartney, whose brilliant songs propelled the Beatles to worldwide sales of 2.3 billion albums. It's true that each of them was creative on his own—after Lennon wrote "Strawberry Fields" during a trip to rural Spain in 1966, McCartney returned the volley in a few days with "Penny Lane"—but it was the partnership that provided the magic. "Distinctions are a good way to introduce ourselves to a creative pair. But what matters is how the parts come together," writes Joshua Wolf Shenk. Lennon's and McCartney's music originated as "single strands" that twisted "into a mutually strengthening double helix."[2]

Shenk cites the marriage expert Dr. John Gottman's principle of "repair"—"a return to the strength of a partnership that tempers the effects of its weaknesses." The Apostle James expressed the same idea somewhat earlier: "Therefore, confess your sins to one another and pray for one another, that you may be healed. The prayer of a righteous person has great power as it is working." (James 5:16) Your marriage is a partnership of disparate personalities, and the way to make such a partnership work is the mutual confession and corporate prayer of two people who have been made righteous by the blood of Christ. The result is a powerful, healed marriage.

Surely your marriage can be a breathtaking rendering of the power of two.

THIRTEEN

A SHEPHERD MEETS THE NEEDS OF HIS SHEEP

My cup overflows.

—PSALM 23:5

For Christians, Palm Sunday is a day for celebration. Perhaps your church, like mine, equips the little kids with palm branches for the processional while the congregation sings "Hosanna, Loud Hosanna." But there was no celebration for me on Palm Sunday of 2015.

Nancy and I had been corresponding for two months. Our first ninety-minute "date" was held in a friend's office in downtown Chicago. We had known each other professionally for a dozen years, but now I was meeting with her for the first time as her friend and possible beau. In that meeting we decided to begin corresponding to "see where the Lord might lead our relationship."

As we prayed and sought godly counsel, we decided to take the three weeks leading up to Easter as a time to fast and pray about the

IN THOSE TWENTY-ONE
DAYS, THIS ROUTINE
BECAME A TREASURED
PERSONAL VISIT TO
THE THRONE.

Lord's direction for our future and whether we were to be together.

Palm Sunday marked the end of the second week of our fast. I had never gone this long without lunch or dinner, but I found it to be a sweet time, humbling myself before the Father and seeking His will. During the lunch hour, I would kneel at a small couch in my bedroom with my Bible, a hymnal, a journal, and a devotional book. In those twenty-one days, this routine became a treasured personal visit to the Throne.

Palm Sunday Panic

On Palm Sunday, I woke up early, and my first conscious thought was one of dread, almost panic. I felt as though I was back in college facing a major exam for which I was not prepared. But I had no idea why.

I made coffee and collected my One Year Bible, my journal, and a protein bar. After an hour or so of studying, writing, and praying, I got ready for church. But the ache in my soul did not go away. Driving to church, I couldn't shake this anguish, try as I might.

My mind in a terrible swirl, I hardly noticed the Palm Sunday service. My heart was racing. I felt as though I had shoplifted merchandise from a jewelry store and was waiting to be arrested, or as though I was sitting in a first-class seat on an airplane with a coach ticket in the seatback pocket, waiting for the flight attendant to ask for my boarding pass. Maybe you've had this feeling.

After church I went straight home. Without stopping to change out of my Sunday clothes, I loosened my tie and went straight to the Throne. I opened my Bible to the twenty-first chapter of John's gospel: "When they had finished breakfast, Jesus said to Simon Peter, 'Simon, son of

John, do you love me more than these?' He said to him, 'Yes, Lord; you know that I love you.' He said to him, 'Feed my lambs.'" (21:15)

In what may have been history's first recorded "Come to Jesus" meeting, the Lord was having a seaside chat with Peter, their first meeting since Judas' betrayal, Peter's denial, and Jesus' trial, crucifixion, and resurrection. Looking directly into the face of the most outspoken of the disciples, Jesus asked Peter, "Do you love me more than these?"

Without warning, those words shed light on the paralyzing emotions I had been experiencing since first opening my eyes that morning. For several weeks, my heart had been swept up in my love for Nancy, which was right and good. But had I allowed this love to eclipse my love for Jesus? What if Jesus were to ask me, "Do you love Me more than Nancy?"

"No," I said aloud. "No, I don't love You more."

In the wake of the most eventful months of my life, I had carelessly allowed my emotions to get the best of me. And in doing this, I was sinning. That day, I did not try to fine-tune my thinking. I did not resolve to do my best to put the Lord back in His rightful place in my heart. No, I confessed my skewed priorities as sin and repented. "Forgive me," I prayed through tears. "I want to love You more. I do love You more. This is Your rightful place."

> IN THE WAKE OF THE MOST HARROWING MONTHS OF MY LIFE, I HAD CARELESSLY ALLOWED MY EMOTIONS TO GET THE BEST OF ME. AND IN DOING THIS, I WAS SINNING.

In my journal I wrote, "Nancy does not belong on the throne of my life. This is raising expectations far beyond her ability to meet my needs. If I put her where she doesn't belong, she will fail." Then I heard Christ's "still, small voice" as clearly as if I had been sitting with him on the shore like Peter: "Feed my lamb."

THE SHEPHERD IN A
MARRIAGE NEEDS TO
UNDERSTAND WHAT HIS
WIFE TRULY LONGS FOR.

Jesus was nudging me with a powerful truth. It was as though He was saying to me, "Listen, Robert. Once you have your affections lined up properly and love me more than anything or anyone, then (and only then) will you be capable of meeting Nancy's needs."

One Size Does Not Fit All

The shepherd in a marriage needs to understand what his wife truly longs for. And when he understands this, then his wife will begin to experience, from a human perspective, "everything she needs." And when it comes to meeting your wife's needs, one size does not fit all.

Since 1985, I have purchased my suits from an Iranian haberdasher in the Los Angeles garment district named Mike, whose clientele ranges from professional athletes to rappers to accountants. But just a few doors down from Mike's is Rollo's tailor shop, and that's where the real magic happens. In that shop, no more than sixteen feet wide and probably seventy feet deep, Rollo welcomes patrons with a Formica countertop, worn to white at the edges, a few dressing rooms with flimsy curtains, and a queue of industrial-strength sewing machines, managed by men and women who run them with surgical precision.

Ten years ago, when I introduced Christopher, my son-in-law, to the garment district, he selected a beautiful Italian suit from Mike's shop, but the pants were pleated, and Christopher wanted plain front. So we walked over to Rollo's and asked him if he could do the complete makeover to Christopher's trousers. "Of course," he replied with a reassuring smile. By the time we returned from a quick lunch, Christopher's trousers were ready. The results were astonishing. The tailoring was flawless, and this suit is still one of Christopher's favorites.

You can't meet your wife's needs by pulling something off the rack at Walmart. What you give her must be tailor-made. You've got to be her Rollo. But how do you do that? How do you figure out what she needs, and how can you tell if you're meeting those needs? Here's how.

Loving Jesus More

Christ is asking you the same question He asked Peter on the seashore—"Do you love Me more than anyone? Or anything?" And you've got to be able to answer as Peter did—"Yes, Lord, I love You more than anyone. Or anything." But how do you know if that answer is true?

At the risk of telling you what you already know, I'll say that you must begin your day with your Shepherd.

Picture yourself in a packed sheepfold at dawn. A naturally light sleeper, you hear the Shepherd's footsteps as He approaches the gate. You perk up your ears and lift your head. Is this your Shepherd? Pushing through your sleepiness, you crawl to your feet and make your way toward Him. The closer you get, the more clearly you see His face. His radiant countenance pierces and dispels the darkness. When you reach Him, He picks you up and carries you to a special place not far from the gate. Your heart races with joy. This is going to be a precious time—just you and your very own Shepherd.

> WHEN YOU REACH HIM, HE PICKS YOU UP AND CARRIES YOU TO A SPECIAL PLACE NOT FAR FROM THE GATE. YOUR HEART RACES WITH JOY. THIS IS GOING TO BE A PRECIOUS TIME—JUST YOU AND YOUR VERY OWN SHEPHERD.

You can actually start every day like that with your Shepherd. Read His Word and meditate on it, write down your thoughts, and finish your time with Him on your knees, thanking Him for His love, His mercy and grace, and then presenting to Him your needs for the day.

But can't this become routine—even boring? Well yes, it can. But so does stepping into the shower or sitting down to a meal. And even though it's the same Bible and the same words you've read before, God can take the ordinary and make it extraordinary. He turns routine into euphoria.

Loving Your Wife Next

Having spent this time with your Shepherd, you're ready to be a shepherd to your wife, to meet her needs. I'm not talking about sentimental Valentine's Day cards or flowers or dinner at her favorite restaurant. These are wonderful, but your sheep is looking for more. If you'll forgive me for stating the obvious, I'd suggest asking your wife what needs she has that you could better meet.

In 2015 I married a woman who had been single for fifty-seven years. Nancy had been making decisions on her own for a long time. Although she had a board of directors, wise senior staffers, and godly colleagues and friends, she didn't have to ask anyone's permission to do anything, especially at home.

A few weeks after I started visiting Nancy's home, I walked past the kitchen sink. Noticing a few dishes in there, I went about rinsing them off and putting them in the dishwasher. Did I do this to impress her? Of course. Did I do this to send a secret message about fastidious neatness? No. A day or two later, I walked past the sink and cleared a few things out again.

> ALTHOUGH SHE HAD A BOARD OF DIRECTORS, WISE SENIOR STAFFERS, AND GODLY COLLEAGUES AND FRIENDS, SHE DIDN'T HAVE TO ASK ANYONE'S PERMISSION TO DO ANYTHING, ESPECIALLY AT HOME.

Then it occurred to me—am I holding the door for the woman at Soukup's hardware store again? I had assumed that Nancy would be happy for me to empty the sink. I mean, who doesn't want an empty kitchen sink? But what if she had her own routine? What if she was thoroughly comfortable with a few stray things in there and planned to empty the sink only once a day after dinner, as normal people do? Would she see my taking this initiative as a gesture of helpfulness or as clinical fastidiousness, an unspoken critique of her housekeeping?

> I NEEDED TO UNDERSTAND HER NEEDS AND TO DO MY BEST TO MEET THEM. *TAILOR-MADE* NEED-MEETING.

So I asked her. "Do you appreciate my clearing the kitchen sink, or would you rather if I'd just leave it?" Simple question, right? But a very important one. My goal, especially because I was trying to win her heart, was to please her. I needed to understand her needs and to do my best to meet them. *Tailor-made* need-meeting.

Making Promises to Your Sheep

When you married your wife, you spoke certain words to her. Standing at the altar, in front of the minister and in the presence of some friends, you spoke. You may have crafted your own covenant or you may have traveled the traditional route. Either way, these words are called wedding vows. Vows are promises. And saying them "before God and these witnesses" to "join this man and this woman" you made them irretractable promises—no less binding than God's pact with Abraham or His rainbowed pledge to Noah. You said to your bride, I give you my word: I will love and cherish you, I will do everything I can to satisfy you. I am serious—dead serious.

And so you set out to meet her needs. To fill her cup so full that it spilled over. You hoped that after a few months of being married, you might overhear her boast to a friend about how well you were

WHEN YOU MARRIED, YOU WERE JOINED TO A CREATURE OF UNIMAGINABLE COMPLEXITY.

doing as her husband, her shepherd. "I can hardly believe it," she would say, "but my husband knows just what I need. The longer we're married, the better he is able to anticipate without my saying anything. His love makes me feel whole. And safe." Or maybe you'd glance at her cellphone and see a text message to her best friend. "Marriage is more amazing than I ever thought it could be. I have never been happier."

Overflowing cup. Mission accomplished.

Watching for Cues

When you married, you were joined to a creature of unimaginable complexity. In you, your wife, on the other hand, probably was not. You'll rarely hear one woman say to another about her husband, "I just can't figure out what he wants. I'm doing my best to meet his needs, but he is so complex, I just don't know where to begin." The perennial lament of men, by contrast, is that they can't figure out what their wives want.

Fortunately, you do not need to become an expert on women in general. As a shepherd, your job is to become skilled at understanding—anticipating—the needs of *just one woman* and then learning the secrets of meeting those needs.

That's all. That's enough.

Time-Tested Principles

There are plenty of good marriage books, many of them written in the past ten or twenty years. But let's return to the amazing 3,500-year-old piece of advice tucked away in the book of Deuteronomy between instructions on divorce and directions for the use of millstones when making a loan agreement. "If a man has recently married, he must not be sent to war or have any other duty laid on him. *For one year* he is to be free to stay at home and bring happiness to his wife he has married." (Deuteronomy 24:5, emphasis added)

However impracticable—even incomprehensible—that counsel may sound, it contains three principles that we ought to take seriously.

1. The Challenge Principle: "One year"

Most guys love a contest. We gravitate toward something competitive. Well, here's a huge challenge. It may be a little late, since you may have been married for longer than a year, but this piece of advice from thousands of years ago is clear: If you want to have a great marriage, don't do anything for a whole year except *learn to love your wife.*

I know what you're saying. "C'mon, be reasonable. I've got work to do. If I had taken a whole year off, I would have been fired from my job, and that wouldn't be good for either one of us."

Or you might be saying, "Hey, this sounds great—a whole year of hanging out with my bride and making love. I could get used to that."

YOUR JOB IS NOT TO BECOME AN EXPERT ON MEETING THE NEEDS OF *ALL* WOMEN. IT IS TO BECOME AN EXPERT ON *ONE* WOMAN—YOUR WIFE.

Whether you think you can't take a year off for history's longest honeymoon or you think it sounds like a lot of fun to take a whole year off to be with your wife—if you could afford it—I have a little something to throw into the mix. As I said, your job is not to become an expert on meeting the needs of *all* women. It is to become an expert on *one* woman—your wife. Neither a weekend seminar, nor a book, nor even the standard five-session premarital counseling commitment is going to be enough.

The primary reason that privately held businesses fail is under-capitalization. Even if you've been married for a long time, if you don't take this challenge of learning about and responding to the needs of your wife, you may have an undercapitalized marriage with no reserves to draw on when things get tough down the road.

2. The Attention Deficit Disorder Principle: "Not be sent to war or have any other duty laid on him"

Many years ago, I learned an important lesson about focused listening. Curiously, the lesson came from watching a deaf person "listen" by way of lip-reading. Here's what I learned: listening is not something you do with your ears; it's something you do with your eyes.

Remember the railroad-crossing sign—stop, look, and listen? Avoiding the distraction of going to war or having other duties laid on you allows you to stop, look, and listen to the wants and the needs of your wife. You are a full-time husband. This is not a part-time or hourly assignment.

SHE SPEAKS TO YOU. YOU HAVE SOMETHING ELSE GOING ON WITH YOUR HANDS OR IN YOUR MIND. YOU HAVE A CHOICE.

The challenge of paying attention presents itself every day—probably several times a day. She speaks to you. You have something else going on with your hands or in your mind. You have a choice. You can stop what you're doing and focus your attention on her, or you can turn away—either physically or emotionally—and keep doing what you're doing.

Focusing on your wife will be a challenge when you have your cellphone in your hand. In my experience, asking if it's okay if I finish the message I'm writing is a good idea. She'll usually say okay. If she doesn't say okay, then it isn't okay. Set your phone down and listen (with your eyes). You can finish the message later, and your wife's confidence in your love for her will expand.

3. The Reciprocity Principle: "Bring happiness to the wife he has married"

Chalk it up to our humanity, but most husbands have this backwards. We're eager for our wives to find ways to make *us* happy.

Early in my marriage to Bobbie, she put it this way: "I just want to know that even though you're busy, once in a while you stop and think about me." "Okay," you might be saying, "but what should my wife do for me?" That's a fair question but the answer is sobering. This Old Testament admonition says absolutely nothing about your wife's job. She's given no direction at all. But this is where the reciprocity part comes in. When you make her happiness your priority, your wife—"the one you have married"—usually finds herself compelled to make *you* happy.

UNHAPPY, NAGGING, CONTENTIOUS, QUARRELSOME WIVES ARE OFTEN MARRIED TO OVERLY-BUSY, UNRESPONSIVE, PREOCCUPIED, SELF-ABSORBED HUSBANDS.

Doing everything you can do to make your wife happy is not just an unselfish act of martyrdom. Having a contented wife will make a difference in your *own* happiness. The Book of Proverbs affirms this truth with a touch of humor—*twice*: "Better to live on a corner of the roof than share a house with a quarrelsome woman." (Proverbs 21:9 and 25:24)

Unhappy, nagging, contentious, quarrelsome wives are often married to overly-busy, unresponsive, preoccupied, self-absorbed husbands. And they've learned by trial and error that the only way they can get their husband's attention is to do one of these annoying things.

Your challenge is to pay more attention to your wife than to your neighbor's new car or the news headlines or the Final Four. When you make this investment, your marriage will be far more satisfying for the rest of your life.[1]

A Quick Lesson from a Quarterback

Becoming an expert on your wife means something else very important. This is a concept that has quite recently dawned on me. Maybe it's because my marriage to Nancy is new and I realize that I have a lot of catching up to do in becoming an expert in knowing her.

I used this word a couple paragraphs ago. The big idea here is *anticipation.*

Imagine a wide receiver in football running a crossing pattern, his body moving quickly across the quarterback's field of vision. When the pass is launched, a seasoned quarterback fires the ball into a void. He does not throw the football to the receiver. He zips it to where his teammate is going to be when the pass arrives. He anticipates. The football and the receiver are supposed to arrive simultaneously.

Unless we're talking about Eddie Murphy in the movie "Dr. Dolittle," your average sheep does not speak. Of course, I'm not suggesting that your wife is somehow incapable of expressing herself. Far from it. But a good shepherd has to know his flock so well that he has the capability of meeting their needs without them asking. The magic here is that you know your wife so well that you slip ahead of her and look for ways to serve her.

"My wife would like water with no ice and a lime, please." When we sit down in a restaurant and the server asks what we'd like to drink, this is what I say. When you notice a trash can that has run out of available space, don't only empty that one but do a quick spin around the house and empty the others. Or when you're sitting on the couch side by side and you see your wife shiver a little, fetch a throw and drape its warmth over her lap and her legs. These things are most fun when they happen without your wife asking. You are anticipating what she needs and you're acting on it. Ask a wife if these kinds of voluntary gestures mean anything to her. She'll likely tell you.

Not a Sure Thing

You're welcome to do your own investigation on this, but I can save you some time and effort. Unless its own baby lamb is threatened, a sheep does not attack. And it will never attack its shepherd. Sheep long to feel safe under the leadership of their shepherd. Although they may wander off, their nature is not to fight or rebel.

Most women want to trust their shepherd. But—and this is an important "but"—their husbands must show themselves trustworthy.

The core message of this book is that you do not have control over your wife's behavior. You did not when you started dating her, you did not when you married her, you do not now. And you never will.

But the really good news is that wives by nature are generally responders. When we lead them with love and grace, they will more often than not respond to us with love and grace. They can't be forced to do this. It is and will always be theirs to choose. That's difficult, because men generally prefer predictability. We like a sure thing. We'd rather ride a Harley than a horse. Twist the grip on the handle, and your motorcycle races off. Spur a horse and it may do the same—or it may throw you into the ditch.

The Art of Wooing and Deep-Sea Fishing

Imagine that you have been invited to go deep-sea fishing. Your host and guide is a veteran angler. He knows where the big ones are and how to land them. You have seen huge marlins mounted on walls and watched videos of guys catching these blue giants. This is exactly what you have in mind this day.

As you're pulling away from the dock, your guide tells you with a chagrined look that he doesn't have the proper fishing line. All he has is twenty-pound test line. There's no guarantee the line won't snap if you hook something big. It could be a few hours before the supplier can bring new line, and you're already some distance from shore, so you decide to go ahead and fish with the line you have. But bringing in the big one without breaking the line will require patience, finesse, and gentleness.

WITH ALL DUE RESPECT TO CUPID, YOU ARE NOT AN ARCHER. YOU ARE A SHEPHERD. YOU ARE HER SHEPHERD.

If she'll forgive this comparison, your wife is a marlin. She's a trophy. You won her when she said "yes" to your proposal of marriage, but now it seems like she's back in the ocean swimming free. You love this woman. You long for her embrace, her heart, her love. But she doesn't want to be yanked, gaffed, and dragged onto the deck of your boat. She longs to be won—to be gently wooed.

Her desire to be romanced is not a game she's playing with you. She's not asking you to jump through one more hoop to prove anything. Wanting to be loved and cherished is in her DNA, just as wanting to win is in yours. You have to win her heart deftly and with skill. You are not spearing it or conquering it. You are not a swashbuckling pirate. You are not a lasso-swinging cowboy. With all due respect to Cupid, you are not an archer. You are a shepherd. You are her shepherd.

Perhaps it's the complexity of understanding and meeting your wife's needs or the deep insecurity every man feels when it comes to many of his primary relationships, but some men are afraid of their wives. Uncertainty about their mate's emotions forces them to live with nagging apprehension. Their insecurity makes them yank on the line and sometimes break it. Instead of winning her, your actions seem to send her away. This estrangement feels like bubbles, gurgling in your gut. You know this bad feeling, don't you?

But it does not need to be this way.

We're going to talk about this challenge in the next chapter. And, to give you a hint, there's good news to be found there. I promise.

FOURTEEN

A SHEPHERD PASTORS HIS SHEEP

There is no fear in love, but perfect love casts out fear. For fear has to do with punishment, and whoever fears has not been perfected in love. We love because he first loved us.

—1 JOHN 4:18–19

Imagine that you were almighty—able to shoot a 59 at Augusta and score thirty-six points in an NBA game. On that deep-sea fishing trip we were imagining in the last chapter, you could simply command your marlin to turn itself in, and it would flip itself up onto the deck. How cool would this be?

Our Good Shepherd Is an Expert in Romance

The amazing truth of our Good Shepherd is that, even though He has the power to do whatever He chooses, He does something else. Just as He could win at Wimbledon or wow the men and women of a joint session of Congress with a speech, He could force you to

AS THE DISCIPLE JOHN PUTS IT, WE LOVE OUR SHEPHERD BECAUSE HE FIRST LOVED US.

love and follow Him. But that's not this Shepherd's way. God has chosen instead to pursue us, to gently tug, entreat, and lead us. He even supernaturally plants in our hearts a desire to know and follow Him. As the disciple John puts it, we love our Shepherd because He first loved us. Or as Aesop might have put it, God warms us by His love and presence, and our hearts are drawn to Him.

The Great Attractor

Speaking of Aesop, here's a story that sounds like one of his fables, but it's not. It's true. In early 2016, scientists using a radio telescope discovered 883 galaxies previously "hidden" from view behind the stars and dust of our own Milky Way. The discovery might explain an anomaly dubbed the Great Attractor—a mysterious region of enormous gravitational force first detected in the 1970s.

The first letter of John depicts God as a Cosmic Romantic, enticing us, courting us, drawing us to Himself. His love is like the mysterious gravitational pull that scientists have been trying to understand. This God Who took the first step toward us is the "Great Attractor."

In the spring of 1738, John Wesley, the leader of the Methodist movement, a young man deeply serious about his Christian faith, recorded in his journal:

> In the evening, I went very unwillingly to a society in Aldersgate Street, where one was reading Luther's preface to the Epistle of the Romans. About a quarter before nine, while he was describing the change which God works in

the heart through faith in Christ, I felt my heart strangely warmed. I felt I did trust in Christ, Christ alone, for salvation; and an assurance was given me that He had taken away my sins, even mine, saved me from the law of sin and death.[1]

Wesley did not write, "I decided to be attracted to Jesus," or "God came along and bonked me on the head, dragging my unconscious body to a place I had no intention of going." Nor did he write, "After years of research and serious consideration, I concluded that following Christ made good sense." No, he wrote, "I felt my heart strangely warmed." He had nothing to do with this warming. Someone else—let's call Him our Good Shepherd—did the charming.

> **JESUS IS THE PERFECT MODEL OF SHEPHERDING, AND THIS IS EXACTLY WHAT YOUR WIFE IS LOOKING FOR IN YOU.**

God the great Romantic—the Great Attractor—takes a smart and religious man like John Wesley and warms his heart. Of course, as He did with the Apostle Paul, God could have thrown him off his horse. Or sent a comet into his bedroom. But as many preachers and theologians have pointed out, "God is usually a gentleman." And a Good Shepherd.

Jesus is the perfect model of shepherding, and this is exactly what your wife is looking for in you.

Leading with Love and Grace, with Humility and Strength

All this talk about winning the heart of our sweetheart might sound weak to you, perhaps even unmanly, as if I were counseling you to plead with your wife, "Please love me. Oh, please, *please* love me. If you don't love me, my heart will be dashed on the rocks!" That's not what I'm talking about *at all*.

If the image of God as the divine suitor doesn't appeal to you, the nineteenth-century poet Francis Thompson offers something very different—divine grace as "The Hound of Heaven" in relentless pursuit of the soul:

> I fled Him, down the nights and down the days;
> I fled Him, down the arches of the years;
> I fled Him, down the labyrinthine ways
> Of my own mind; and in the midst of tears
> I hid from Him, and under running laughter.

But whether you think of God as the Great Attractor or the Hound of Heaven, He's always the Good Shepherd who leads his sheep. You pursued the woman who became your wife, and I hope you still do. But when you became her husband, you became her shepherd, and that means leading.

CLEARLY, THE IDEA OF A MAN LEADING HIS WIFE UPSETS MANY PEOPLE. THEY THINK IT SMACKS OF CHAUVINISM, MACHISMO. NO, THIS IS NOT WHAT THIS LOOKS LIKE.

Clearly, the idea of a man leading his wife upsets many people. They think it smacks of chauvinism, machismo. No, this is not what this looks like.

By His grace, in my lifetime, God has given me the privilege of being married to two strong, capable, skilled, and gifted women. In many ways, they were smarter and more talented than I could have ever aspired to be. It would have been easy to be intimidated by Bobbie and Nancy. But these women chose to embrace the biblical directive to submit to me, to respect me, and to "let me lead." And because they did, two things happened.

Stepping Up

First, I stepped up. I felt the slap of the baton in my hand, and I did my best to run with confidence. Bobbie trusted me; Nancy trusts me. And that trust changes everything.

My model has been the Good Shepherd. He loved me and gave Himself for me. The Apostle Paul, in a famous passage, describes this flawless leadership:

> Have this mind among yourselves, which is yours in Christ Jesus, who, though he was in the form of God, did not count equality with God a thing to be grasped, but emptied himself, by taking the form of a servant, being born in the likeness of men. And being found in human form, he humbled himself by becoming obedient to the point of death, even death on a cross. (Philippians 2:5–8)

Leadership in my marriage has meant humbly swallowing pride and serving. For a man who is a card-carrying sinner, who would rather have it his way, this is a huge challenge. Again, Paul describes this precisely:

> For I know that nothing good dwells in me, that is, in my flesh. For I have the desire to do what is right, but not the ability to carry it out. For I do not do the good I want, but the evil I do not want is what I keep on doing. Now if I do what I do not want, it is no longer I who do it, but sin that dwells within me. (Romans 7:18–20)

Like Webb Simpson walking down the seventeenth fairway at Olympic just before winning the U.S. Open, I may sound like I'm

> SHE INVITED ME TO LEAD AND SHE PROSPERED. SHE SUBMITTED TO HER EARTHLY SHEPHERD AND SHE WAS SATISFIED—AND HAPPY.

boasting, but I'm really admitting how inadequate I am for the responsibilities of a shepherd. My eyes are not on myself, a distinctly flawed and imperfect man, but, by necessity and sheer panic, fixed on Jesus, the foundation of my faith (Hebrews 12:1–2).

Flourishing

The second thing that happened when my wife let me lead was that she flourished. That may sound counterintuitive. She invited me to lead and she prospered. She submitted to her earthly shepherd and she was satisfied—and happy.

There wasn't a lot in Bobbie's own background to give her confidence in male leadership, so it was a big step—a leap of faith, actually—for her to take the Bible seriously and submit to her husband's leadership. But that act of faith gave her a renewed joy of loving me and serving others.

Bobbie's funeral service closed with a video of her walking on the street in front our Orlando home (I took the video from the balcony with my smartphone without her knowledge) and singing one of her favorite hymns, which so clearly summarizes this special relationship that we both shared with our Savior, our Good Shepherd.

> When we walk with the Lord
> In the light of His Word,
> What a glory He sheds on our way.
> While we do His good will
> He abides with us still
> And with all who will trust and obey.

Leading

When I married Nancy, she already had a lifetime of accomplishments: eighteen books with sales in excess of three million copies, head of an international ministry, host of a daily radio program broadcast on eight hundred stations. She led conferences attended by tens of thousands of women. Nancy's reputation was heroic and her ministry was highly respected. Not only that, she was completely satisfied in her calling as a single woman. She never expected to be married and, as she told me after our engagement, had never even prayed for a husband. If ever there was a woman who needed a man "like a fish needs a bicycle," it was Nancy.

> BUT FOR DECADES, NANCY'S MESSAGE TO WIVES WAS THE SAME AS BOBBIE'S. "TRUST GOD. SUBMIT TO YOUR HUSBAND. LET HIM LEAD."

But for decades, Nancy's message to wives was the same as Bobbie's. "Trust God. Submit to your husband. Let him lead." And so when the curtain went up on her own wedding day, that's exactly what she did. No, she did not lose her identity. She did not melt onto the kitchen floor or fade into the wallpaper. But she embraced me as her husband, her shepherd. She trusted God, submitted herself to me, and she let me lead.

Can you imagine?

Your Very Own Flock

In Chapter Twelve we talked about being the priest—the pastor—in our marriages and homes. This is clearly the role God has given to us. You may have a bunch of children or it may just be you and your wife, but if you're the shepherd that means those under your care are your flock.

Even though we've been talking about this from the beginning, I want you to form a mental picture of yourself as an actual shepherd.

Go ahead—include the headdress, the bathrobe, the hooked staff, and the rod hanging from the sash around your waist. You're standing in a meadow; a soft and pleasant breeze is brushing against your face. And you're looking over your flock. You're even welcome to place your dog in the picture, although he may not be adept at a sheepdog's duties. Like my little white Maltese, he may be functionally incompetent and just fascinated with the sheep. That's okay—you can leave him in the picture.

OUR MEALS BEGIN THE SAME WAY JESUS' MEALS MUST HAVE BEGUN, GIVING THANKS TO THE LORD FOR THE FOOD.

Take a deep breath. You are the shepherd. And these sheep are your charge. They are your flock. Go ahead; drink this in.

In his first epistle, the Apostle Peter offers a wonderfully clear summary of your task—a shepherd's job description:

> So I exhort the elders[2] among you, as a fellow elder and a witness of the sufferings of Christ, as well as a partaker in the glory that is going to be revealed: shepherd the flock of God that is among you, exercising oversight, not under compulsion, but willingly, as God would have you; not for shameful gain, but eagerly; not domineering over those in your charge, but being examples to the flock. And when the chief Shepherd appears, you will receive the unfading crown of glory. Likewise, you who are younger, be subject to the elders. Clothe yourselves, all of you, with humility toward one another, for "God opposes the proud but gives grace to the humble." (1 Peter 5:1–4)

Without taking too much time and space, let me unpack this amazing assignment, unapologetically given to us as shepherds from the pages of God's Holy Word.

A Fellow Shepherd and Witness
to Christ's Sufferings

Peter is inviting us to join him as a fellow elder and witness—an eyewitness. One of Jesus' closest friends, Peter knew what he was talking about. He was part of the Good Shepherd's flock and saw him under almost every conceivable circumstance. So the next few sentences are not just theory, they're truth hammered out on the anvil of real life under the leadership of the Shepherd.

Partaker in Glory

The word "partaker" suggests eating meals together, as in "You prepare a table before me." As part of our Shepherd's flock, we regularly receive invitations to share a meal with Him. This is not an exclusive, members-only club. This is a gathering of friends, with Jesus as host.

As I have said, regular mealtimes with your wife should be a non-negotiable. This would not be the first time that I've been accused of being a micromanager, but in a restaurant, when it's just the two of us, I always try to find a square table where we can sit across the corner from each other. Even at a fast-food place, this placement is my favorite. Because we don't have a whole table between us, we can turn our chairs toward each other and slide them close. And our meals begin the same way Jesus' meals must have begun, giving thanks to the Lord for the food. And I always thank Him for this amazing and precious person I get to hold hands and eat this meal—and do life—with.

Shepherd the flock of God
that is among you

In the kind of direct statement that we'd expect from Peter, we are given clear instructions. If this passage had been written out as a headline for an ad, it would simply say, "Be the Shepherd."

IF SOMEONE HAD TOLD YOU A FEW DAYS AGO THAT AS A HUSBAND, YOU WERE RESPONSIBLE TO "PASTOR AND SHEPHERD" YOUR WIFE, YOU MIGHT HAVE STARED BACK AT HIM IN PUZZLEMENT.

And then, in order to help us understand how to approach our assignment, he gives us some additional directions. "Not under compulsion but willingly"—not because you *have* to but because you *want* to. "Not for shameful gain but eagerly"—our marriages are not about us. "Not domineering over those in your charge"—gentle, gentle, gentle. But being an example to the flock—the shepherd always goes first and shows the way.

"And when the chief Shepherd appears, you will receive the unfading crown of glory"—our Good Shepherd is here in spirit, and some day He is coming back. When He does, we want Him to see what kind of shepherd we have been and say, "Well done, good and faithful servant—man, husband, father…shepherd." (Matthew 25:21)

Cutting to the Chase

I want to challenge you to "pastor" your wife well. You are the shepherd of your flock, small or large. If someone had told you a few days ago that as a husband, you were responsible to "pastor and shepherd" your wife, you might have stared back at him in puzzlement. My hope is that you now have a greater sense of what pastoring and shepherding mean. But as important as it is to understand your job description, something else is necessary.

Let me tell you a story about a man with whom you and I may be able identify. It's a true story, recorded in three of the Gospels (Matthew 19:16–24, Mark 10:17–31, Luke 18:18–23). One day a man approached Jesus, eager to speak directly to Him. In fact, he ran to meet him, something only desperate people do.

The disciples may have recognized him—he was a man of some standing in the community—or he may have been so self-assured that he simply pushed his way through the crowd to get directly in front of the Savior, but when he reached Jesus, he fell down humbly on his knees.

This fellow seems to have had it all. All three Gospel accounts tell us that he was rich, and Matthew adds that he was young. By his own account—which Jesus did not dispute—he was morally upright as well, having kept all the commandments from his youth. His rectitude had been recognized when he was made the chief of a synagogue. Who wouldn't want to be like this guy?

But deep in his heart there seems to have lurked a fear that he did not have what mattered most: salvation, eternal life, and the hope of heaven.[3] Rising to his feet, the young man asked what seems like a reasonable question: "Good Teacher, what must I do to inherit eternal life?"

Having considered our role as shepherd of our marriage and family, let's put ourselves in this young man's place. Our question of the Good Shepherd might be, "Good Teacher, what must I do to be a good shepherd?"

> JESUS' ANSWER TO THE RICH YOUNG MAN MAY SEEM CONFUSING TO US. HE TOLD HIM THAT HE NEEDED TO HAVE A BIG GARAGE SALE AND GET RID OF HIS STUFF.

Jesus' answer to the rich young man may seem confusing to us. He told him that he needed to have a big garage sale and get rid of his stuff. That doesn't sound very spiritual. Wouldn't it be better to tell him to take this little booklet, pray this prayer, and *voilà*, you're in? What's the deal with unloading your possessions?

Tailor-Made Invitations

Jesus' response to the rich young man is the only instance in the Gospels in which He tells someone to sell all his material possessions in order to follow Him. Jesus told Nicodemus, a man proud of his high position among the Jews, that he needed to be "born again" (John 3:7). He told that Samaritan woman at the well, a person who lived to please her senses, that she needed to drink deeply of "living water" (John 4:10). And to the thief hanging on the cross next to Him—precariously suspended in mid air—a man clearly out of options, who simply begged Jesus, "Remember me"—Jesus responded, "Today you will be with me in Paradise" (Luke 23:43). In other words, "You're in, friend. Welcome to the family."

THE SIGHT OF HER HUSBAND ON HIS KNEES BEFORE HIS HEAVENLY FATHER MAY BE THE MOST ATTRACTIVE THING YOUR WIFE WILL EVER SEE.

Like the rich young man, you and I approach the Good Shepherd. We walk, we jog, or we run. And when we arrive in his holy presence, we go to our knees with the question, "Good Shepherd, what must I do to be a good shepherd?"

I don't know what your greatest need is. I don't know if you need to be "born again," or to drink some of that "living water" or if you're simply crying out, "Save me, I'm dying here." Our sinfulness, our shame, our inability to be the shepherd our wife wants and needs is enough. Jesus looks into our eyes and says, "Believe in Me. Trust in Me. I'm the Good Shepherd. Follow Me."

The invitation—the Gospel—is clear. It's exactly what you and I need. And the first lesson we learned from the successful young man who came to Jesus is a good one. We start this conversation on our knees.

The sight of her husband on his knees before his Heavenly Father may be the most attractive thing your wife will ever see. You can run fast. You can hit a golf ball three hundred yards. You can build a deck on the back of your house or mend a leaky faucet. You can have the right answer for every question she asks. But none of these things compares with the flip of her heart when she sees you seeking and submitting to your Shepherd.

LOVE FOR A LIFETIME: FINISHING WELL

Till death do us part.

O ne day you looked into the face of your bride and you repeated these words: "Till death do us part." Your mind may have been elsewhere. You may have been so nervous or tired or preoccupied with the pleasures to come that you weren't paying much attention. But despite the distractions, you made this vow.

The interesting thing about this promise is that you had no idea how long you were binding yourself. You don't know how long you have to live, and you don't know how old your wife will be when she breathes her last. Your goal is to make it to the end, to stay faithful, strong, even happy and pleased with your marriage until the day one of you buries the other.

Not Running Out of Fuel

When I was growing up, the Indianapolis 500 was a big deal, especially in our house, where my dad was a consummate car guy. It became my Memorial Day ritual to listen to the race on the radio (it wasn't broadcast live on television until 1986) while washing and waxing the family car. As I recall, I began this tradition in 1961, when A. J. Foyt won his first Indy and I was thirteen. I couldn't drive the car on the street, but I was plenty adept at maneuvering it from the garage to a good spot on the driveway for its treatment.

> YOUR GOAL IS TO MAKE IT TO THE END, TO STAY FAITHFUL, STRONG, EVEN HAPPY AND PLEASED WITH YOUR MARRIAGE UNTIL THE DAY ONE OF YOU BURIES THE OTHER.

What I loved most about the "Greatest Spectacle in Racing" was the way the driver and the pit crew worked as a team. In those days there was no electronic communication between driver and crew chief, so the guys in the pit had to "talk" to the driver by holding up a large chalkboard, often communicating a message about fuel. "Two laps of gas!" they might tell him. Buffing out the wax on the family car, I would imagine myself in the driver's seat—hoping against hope that I had enough to make it to the finish line.

Your marriage has a fuel tank too. The day you were married, it was full. You couldn't imagine loving your bride more than you did that day. Just the thought of being with her provoked a rush of pure adrenaline. You held her affectionately and spoke to her with the tenderness of a shepherd. But in time "the cares of the world...and the desire for other things" (Mark 4:19) began slowly to drain your tank. A heated argument here, a misunderstanding there; a thoughtless word here, a selfish act there; a critical attitude here, a sharp rejoinder there...and your marriage is running on empty.

Fill 'er Up

In the days before self-service gas stations, a thin air pressure hose lying across the driveway in front of the pump made a bell ring when you drove over it, alerting the attendant that a customer had pulled up. He would hustle out to your car, and you'd roll your window down and tell him, "Fill 'er up."

That may not sound like much of a prayer, but when your joy is drying up, your affections are parched, and your marriage's fuel tank is running low, it's the right thing to say to your Good Shepherd. "Dear Father in Heaven. I'm empty. I need you." It's an admission that your own resources are waning and you know where to go to be filled again.

In the winter of 1926, a Presbyterian minister from Lumberton, South Carolina, named Daniel Iverson was attending a tent revival in Orlando, Florida. On his own, and apparently inspired by an evangelistic sermon on the power of the Holy Spirit, he found his way to the piano at the First Presbyterian Church, where he penned the lyrics of a simple hymn, voicing the plea to be refilled:

A HEATED ARGUMENT HERE, A MISUNDERSTANDING THERE; A THOUGHTLESS WORD HERE, A SELFISH ACT THERE; A CRITICAL ATTITUDE HERE, A SHARP REJOINDER THERE ... AND YOUR MARRIAGE IS RUNNING ON EMPTY.

> Spirit of the Living God,
> Fall afresh on me.
> Break me, melt me, mold me, fill me.
> Spirit of the Living God,
> Fall afresh on me.[1]

Break me
The word "break" in this hymn is used in the sense of breaking a wild horse—not a pleasant experience for animal or man. But if

A LUMP OF SOFT CLAY SLAMMED ONTO THE POTTER'S WHEEL HAS NO WILL OF ITS OWN BUT SUBMITS TO THE SKILLED HANDS OF THE POTTER.

the horse is to be useful, this breaking is essential. This is a picture of you and me that needs no caption.

Melt me

Away with pretense and pride. As the children sing, "I am weak but He is strong." I stand before the Lord and recognize my sinfulness and my desperate need for Him. Actually, it's worse than that—I'm dead. This isn't a makeover. It's a resurrection.

Mold me

A lump of soft clay slammed onto the potter's wheel has no will of its own but submits to the skilled hands of the potter. As the wheel spins, the potter shapes the clay, if it is malleable, into something beautiful and useful.

Fill me

We're back at the gas station, or as my grandpa used to call it, the "filling station." Exactly.

One Last Metaphor, the Greatest One of All

Before the dawn of time, in anticipation of forming the first man and the first woman, the Creator of the universe painted a portrait of His relationship with them. He was the holy and perfect Bridegroom. The human race was to be His bride.

In a vision, the Apostle John—the "disciple whom Jesus loved"—described this wedding: "And I saw the holy city, new Jerusalem, coming down out of heaven from God, prepared as a bride adorned for her husband." (Revelation 21:2)

You are your wife's shepherd. You lovingly know, speak to, satisfy, lead, protect, comfort, feed, encourage, meet the needs of, and pastor your lamb. And together, you and your wife prepare yourselves to be the Good Shepherd's precious bride, looking forward to the wedding of all weddings, when our Bridegroom will come to claim us as His own.

In Chapter Seven I mentioned the way Nancy and I chose to symbolize this moment in our wedding. Her brother escorted her halfway down the aisle, where they stopped, and I began walking toward her. Rather than waiting for her to arrive at the front of the church where I was waiting, like the Good Shepherd does for you and me, I strode—I wanted to run—to meet my bride.

> **"GOING FIRST" IS THE MESSAGE OF THIS BOOK. ANTICIPATING ALL OUR NEEDS. IT'S WHAT OUR GOOD SHEPHERD DOES FOR US.**

"Going first" is the message of this book. Anticipating all our needs. It's what our Good Shepherd does for us. In a message scrawled across the expanses of the cosmos, He shouts to us, "Before you knew Me, I loved you. Before you were even conceived, I knew your name. And I called you to be Mine." (Jeremiah 1:5)

Each day, inspired by our Shepherd's initiative, you step forward to claim your bride, overcoming any timidity or fear, pushing past a culture that may try to intimidate you or keep you from taking this all-out risk.

Willing to love her to the point of sacrificing yourself for her, you claim your bride as your own. You are her shepherd—to protect, to love, to honor, to cherish. Forever.

You're Good to Go ... The Joy of Surrendering to Your Shepherd

How remarkable that Jesus should perform His first miracle at a wedding reception (John 2:1–11). It is a great story of surrendering to our Good Shepherd and being the recipient of His lavish grace.

You'd think that the Creator of the universe and the Savior of the world would have opted for a more spectacular debut—perhaps a tempest calmed or a mass healing. Instead, Jesus turned ordinary water into fine wine to save the father of the bride from embarrassment. Too many guests, too little merlot. That was it.

But if we read closely, we find there's more to the story. The Gospel account follows Jesus' calling of His first disciples and His first recorded direct instructions. As a shepherd would say to his flock,

Jesus said to Peter, Andrew, Philip, and Nathanael, "Follow me." And they did.

Now Jesus, His mother, and these new followers are attending a wedding in the tiny village of Cana, just about a mile north of Nazareth in Galilee. Mary, noticing like a good Jewish mother that the wine has run short, brings the problem to her son's attention: "They have no wine." Seeing six stone water pots standing nearby, Jesus issues His second recorded directive, telling the servants, "Fill the jars with water." They obey, filling them to the brim. Without fanfare, Jesus then tells them to "draw some out, and take it to the steward of the feast," who discovers that the jars are full of the finest wine.

Jesus performed this miracle in the presence of the men who had just begun to follow Him, demonstrating what abundant, lavish grace looks like—almost 180 gallons of it. Jesus calls us too to follow Him. For us, this is a big decision. With all our hearts, we hope it's a good decision. And then, as He did with His disciples, Jesus gives us a taste of what following Him will be like. It may be something dramatic (see above) or just a quiet nudge in the night. "You've done the right thing," a still, small voice may whisper. "I will be a Good Shepherd. You are safe. I know you. You can follow Me. You can trust Me."

In the thirty-fourth Psalm, David, the shepherd-king, rejoices in this special companionship with the Good Shepherd: "Oh, taste and see that the LORD is good! Blessed is the man who takes refuge in him!" In this Psalm that follows just a few pages after the "Shepherd's Psalm," David gives us a hint at what following the Lord was going to be like. The Lord was David's Shepherd. He's also yours. And mine.

More than Mere Poetry

There's a story, often told, of a famous actor who gave an after-dinner speech. In the version of the story I know, the actor asked his audience if they would like him to recite a poem. There was silence until an old vicar raised his hand and called out, "Psalm Twenty-three, please." The actor agreed on the condition that the pastor himself should also recite the Psalm after him.

The actor went first, flawlessly reciting the Shepherd's Psalm. Dramatic inflection and theatrical pauses highlighted the polished recitation. When the actor finished, he received enthusiastic applause. Acknowledging the acclamation with a gracious bow, he then gestured toward the minister. The old man walked carefully to the podium and slowly, deliberately, from his heart recited the Psalm:

> The LORD is my shepherd; I shall not want.
>
> He maketh me to lie down in green pastures: he leadeth me beside the still waters.
>
> He restoreth my soul: he leadeth me in the paths of righteousness for his name's sake.
>
> Yea, though I walk through the valley of the shadow of death, I will fear no evil: for thou art with me; thy rod and thy staff they comfort me.
>
> Thou preparest a table before me in the presence of mine enemies: thou anointest my head with oil; my cup runneth over.
>
> Surely goodness and mercy shall follow me all the days of my life: and I will dwell in the house of the LORD forever.

When he finished, the minister carefully made his way back to his place and sat down. An almost holy hush swept across the large room. The actor, as moved as the rest of the audience, returned to the podium. After a few moments, he gathered his brimming emotions. "Do you know the difference between my version of the twenty-third Psalm and his?" He did not wait for an answer. "I memorized this psalm. I learned it in acting school. I have recited this classic many times before audiences like you." He paused, looking kindly at the minister. "I know the psalm," he said. "But you, my friend, know the Shepherd."

Never Too Late

Nancy and I have a close friend whose parents never attended church or acknowledged any interest in things of God. As she grew older, she would tell and retell her mother the story of Jesus and His redeeming love. "This is fine for weak people," her mother would retort, "but I'm strong."

Not long ago, our friend's mother was stricken with a terminal illness. Her daughter stayed at her bedside, singing and reciting Scripture, including Psalm twenty-three. Presently, she told her daughter, "Now I am weak."

"You know the Gospel as well as I do," our friend told her mother. "But I don't think you know the Shepherd."

"You're right," the old woman replied. "Would you tell me about Him?" And there, just days before her mother drew her final breath, this daughter had the great joy of introducing her mother to the Good Shepherd.

You and I are weak. If we set our pride and pretense aside, we know how weak we are. We need a shepherd. We need the Shepherd.

You know about Him.

Now you can know Him.

Benediction

This is one of my favorite "final words" in the Bible. Can we envision this prayer being spoken over you and me, men who have been called to lead—and to follow?

"Now may the God of peace who brought again from the dead our Lord Jesus, the great Shepherd of the sheep, by the blood of the eternal covenant, equip you with everything good that you may do His will, working in us that which is pleasing in His sight, through Jesus Christ, to whom be glory forever and ever. Amen." (Hebrews 13:20–21)

How to Embrace the Good Shepherd as Your Good Shepherd

When you walk into a huge mall, you're usually greeted by a big, lighted box that features the layout of the mall. If you're looking for a suitcase or a pair of shoes or a gift for your wife, you can find the right store in the directory. But before you set off for your destination, there's something important you must do first. You need to find the little marker on the map that says "You are here."

Once you have that spot identified, you can strike out in the right direction.

Getting Saved

Perhaps you equate the expression "getting saved" with the old circuit-riding preachers who traveled from town to town asking people, "Are you saved?"

PERHAPS YOU
AND NATHAN HAVE
SOMETHING IN COMMON.
COULD IT BE THAT
YOU KNOW *ABOUT* THE
GOOD SHEPHERD, BUT
YOU DON'T *KNOW* THE
GOOD SHEPHERD?

You may even wince at the directness of these words. They sound archaic. But when you're lifeless at the bottom of the ocean—and if you don't know Jesus as your Shepherd, you are dead (Ephesians 2:1)—you don't need a motivational speech or a cute illustration. You don't even need a life preserver thrown from the deck of a ship. You have perished. You're room temperature. Like a bewildered shopper in the mall, you need to find out where you are. You need a Savior.

A few months ago, I received a "911" text from a close friend asking me to call as soon as possible. I had known Nathan for several years. He had grown up attending church and knew quite a bit about Jesus and salvation. But the wheels were coming off his business, and he was desperate. I called immediately, and when he answered he began to cry. I held on until he could gather his composure. Then he filled me in on what was happening.

After a few minutes of conversation about more than his business struggle—about his heart and the major crisis there—I asked Nathan if he would like "to invite Jesus to save him."

"Yes, I would," my friend replied. For the next twenty minutes or so, I helped him walk from death into life. At the close of our phone call, Nathan and I prayed. He confessed his sin and need for a Savior, and then he invited Jesus—his Savior, his Shepherd—to come into his life and save him.

Perhaps you and Nathan have something in common. Could it be that you know *about* the Good Shepherd, but you don't *know* the Good Shepherd? You can invite Him into your life right now, just as Nathan did.

When Hell Breaks Loose

Several years ago, I wrote a book titled *Seven Things You Better Have Nailed Down before All Hell Breaks Loose*. If you're where Nathan was when he sent me the "911" message, maybe what I had to say there will be helpful.

Hell breaks loose in different ways. For Nathan, it was a business disaster. For you it may be a medical diagnosis or serious trouble in your marriage. And crises arise for different reasons. Sometimes our troubles are the result of foolish decisions we made ourselves. Jesus' parable of the Prodigal Son (Luke 15:11–32) is the story of someone who hit bottom because of his own choices. He brought it on himself.

But hell can also break loose because of someone else's foolish choice. Some people staring into the barrel of a gun are victims of other people's misdeeds. A woman once sat in our living room pouring out to Bobbie her painful story of physical and emotional abuse at the hands of her father, which left terrible scars. Her tragic story calls to mind the parable of the lost coin (Luke 15:8–10). Coins do not have the will or the capability to get lost. They don't crawl away to some undisclosed location under their own power. But because of the negligence of their owners, they can be misplaced. Their problems are not of their own making.

Then again, hell can break loose because of an unexpected tragedy. The daily news is filled with stories of devastation and chaos: "Tornadoes Rip through Midwest, 15 Dead," "School Principal Shot," "ISIS Violence Escalates, Christians Beheaded." Sometimes the Internet isn't the only source of fear. You are stricken with a life-threatening illness. Your friend's child is seriously injured in an automobile accident. Your house is burglarized. Someone who receives a cancer diagnosis or finds himself in the path of an out-of-control car might not have made any foolish choices, but the trauma he faces is no less striking.

SOMEONE HAS WISELY SAID THAT IT DOESN'T MATTER WHAT HAPPENS TO US; IT'S WHAT *HAPPENS* TO WHAT HAPPENS TO US THAT REALLY MATTERS.

Sometimes it's useful to identify the reason for the crisis you are facing. But as tempting as it is to spend time analyzing the whys and wherefores, there is danger in getting stuck there. Dwelling on something in the past that we cannot control or change is counterproductive. The "if onlys" of our foolish choices or acrimony toward those at fault will not help with what we are facing right now. And grousing about our predicament or insisting on our innocence doesn't transform us.

Someone has wisely said that it doesn't matter what happens to us; it's what *happens* to what happens to us that really matters. The origin of the tragedy—the reason for hell's breaking loose—may be interesting to talk about over coffee with your closest friend. But what we *do* at the moment is what matters.

The Apostle Paul settles the issue of looking back: "Forgetting those things which are behind and reaching forward to those things which are ahead, I press toward the goal for the prize of the upward call of God in Christ Jesus." (Philippians 3:13–14) It might be tempting to call Paul an out-of-touch idealist. He's not, because he precedes his counsel with this: "I do not regard myself as having laid hold of it yet; but one thing I do…" (3:13a)

Predictably, this determination not to dwell on the past is challenging. It's tough to let go of bitterness or regret. Yet what does Paul decide? He decides to *do* something: "this thing I *do*!" I *will* forget the past.

When hell breaks loose, it peels back the cover to reveal exactly who we are. C. S. Lewis wrote, "Surely what a man does when he is taken off his guard is the best evidence for what sort of man he is."[1]

How well we do when all hell breaks loose depends on one thing: how well we prepare for it *right now*, long before the devastation arrives. Having the essentials in place—nailing them down—can prepare us for anything. It is something we can *do*.

When the moment comes—and it *will* come for us—and your heart pounds with indescribable panic, the seven things you have nailed down will provide solace and confidence. Like a steel beam under a heavy load, these rock-solid biblical truths will sustain you. Having built a godly interior life will have been the *best* preparation.

> LIKE THE SECURITY A CHILD FEELS AS SHE GRASPS HER FATHER'S HAND, THE ASSURANCE THAT WE ARE NOT ALONE IS A GIFT FROM THE GREAT "I AM." HE IS HERE, AND HE IS IN CHARGE.

So here are some things to nail down…truths to learn…truths that provide exactly what we need.

Let's consider these seven things one at a time.

1. God is God

The news God delivered from the burning bush to an insecure and fearful Moses is still true. "I AM who I AM," God said. He might have added, "And you're not."

Like the security a child feels as she grasps her father's hand, the assurance that we are not alone is a gift from the great "I AM." He is here, and He is in charge. In tragic times, the fact that God is God provides us with more sanctuary than we can imagine…and it's just what we need.

Like a parent watching a child on the playground, God is always looking after us with a loving eye. He is God. "God is our refuge and strength, always ready to help in times of trouble. So we will not fear, even if earthquakes come and the mountains crumble into the sea." (Psalm 46:1–2, NLT)

God is the Creator

It's great assurance when tragedy strikes that God made us. "We are His workmanship," Paul tells us (Ephesians 2:10). He could have added, "There's nothing about us that He doesn't know and love."

The book you're holding right now is a "made thing." As you sit reading it, there will never be a moment of doubt that *someone* printed its pages and bound them into a book. If you look up from this page, you'll see more "made things." Fabrics, furniture, light fixtures. If someone tried to convince you that any of these just appeared without a designer and builder, you would laugh.

You and I are "made things" too. Our eyes, our limbs, our internal organs were custom-built, made to order—by God. He knows all about us physically.

AND NOT ONLY DID HE MAKE YOU AND ME, BUT THE VASTNESS OF THE UNIVERSE IS ALSO GOD'S CREATION, SET IN PLACE BY HIS COMMAND.

Not only did He create our physiques, but God also designed our emotions—the euphoria and satisfaction we feel, as well as anxiety and anger and panic. He understands them. Not a single feeling that we experience surprises Him. He made us.

And not only did He make you and me, but the vastness of the universe is also God's creation, set in place by His command. The brilliance of the sunset and the panoply of stars that follow, hawks that circle overhead without flapping their wings, and the delicate petals of the wildflowers in the field across from your house...all of these are His doing.

God is Holy

Although words like *perfect* and *clean* and *set apart* may help us envision what "holy" means, they still fall short. God's holiness, His faultlessness, is a mystery that cannot be fully explained or comprehended.

It was God's holiness that overwhelmed men and women in the Bible, sending them to the ground on their faces in His breathtaking presence. Imagine how you would feel if you walked into the kitchen tomorrow morning and Jesus Christ was sitting at the table, stirring a fresh cup of tea and waiting for you. You would be overwhelmed. Completely speechless. The experience of seeing His magnificence would be more than you could take. The Bible is filled with stories of people who were overcome simply by being in God's holy presence.

THE BIBLE IS FILLED WITH STORIES OF PEOPLE WHO WERE OVERCOME SIMPLY BY BEING IN GOD'S HOLY PRESENCE.

When trouble comes, a holy God is the most qualified specialist in the cosmos. His perfection is sure. Knowing His character and relying on who His is when crisis comes brings inexpressible security. He is eternity's best. No one—no *thing*—is His equal. God is holy.

God is Sovereign

God is active and participates in His creation, twenty-four hours a day, seven days a week. He didn't just make our bodies; His involvement continues moment after moment. He turns our food into fuel. When we inhale, He tells our bodies exactly what to do with the air we've just taken in. When our kids scrape their knees, His healing power goes into action and creates a scab so the wound has a protective covering. And after falling into bed completely depleted at the end of an exhausting day, we wake up the next morning feeling rested

OF ALL OF GOD'S
ATTRIBUTES, HIS
MERCY IS THE MOST
COMFORTING, ESPECIALLY
WHEN CALAMITY
KNOCKS AT OUR DOOR.

because He restored us during the night. These actions are part of God's *ongoing* creative miracle in our bodies.

And God is involved in the activities and events of our lives...and in the world. He knows about everything. And He grants His personal consent and orders its sequence. Sometimes His permission includes those things that look like hell breaking loose. But as awful as the moment may seem to us, God is never surprised. Never. He knew this was coming. He has already been there.

He made us, and He's still involved.

God is Merciful

Of all of God's attributes, His mercy is the most comforting, especially when calamity knocks at our door. God's presence is comforting. His holiness lifts our esteem for Him. We stand in wonder at His creation. And His sovereignty assures us that life is not random and meaningless. But it's God's mercy that fills our hearts with confidence.

King David, who knew something about hell breaking loose, sang of this assurance in Psalm 103:

> The LORD is merciful and gracious;
> He is slow to get angry and full of unfailing love.
> He will not constantly accuse us,
> Nor remain angry forever.
> He has not punished us for all our sins,
> Nor does he deal with us as we deserve.
> For his unfailing love toward those who fear him
> Is as great as the height of the heavens above the earth.
> He has removed our rebellious acts

As far away from us as the east is from the west.
The LORD is like a father to his children,
Tender and compassionate to those who fear him.
For he understands how weak we are;
He knows we are only dust.

Although God has the right and the power to be merciless, especially when our disaster is of our own making, He is filled with love. He is sympathetic and patient with us.

The first thing to nail down is that God is God. This lays the foundation for being ready.

2. The Bible is God's Word

With over thirty billion copies in print, the Bible is the best-selling book of all time. And best-selling books sell because of what? Buzz— people excitedly telling each other about them.

It was my privilege to grow up in a home where the Bible was valued, but the stories I read from *Foxe's Book of Martyrs* as a kid gave me a special reverence for God's Word. Real people—dads, moms, and kids—were burned at the stake because they refused to stop translating, printing, distributing, or reading the Bible. They would not deny its truth.

Persecution has not disappeared. Not long ago, forty-one-year-old Abdul Rahman was arrested by Afghan authorities and sentenced to die. His crime? He owned a Bible. Most experts agreed that, without the outcry from the countries who had sacrificed to free Afghanistan, Rahman would have been beheaded. As it turned out, he was freed and immediately exiled to Italy on the grounds that he was mentally ill.

Nothing in Afghanistan was more dangerous than owning a copy of the Bible, including the possession of illegal drugs or explosives.

WITH OVER THIRTY BILLION COPIES IN PRINT, THE BIBLE IS THE BEST-SELLING BOOK OF ALL TIME.

Why is this true? Because nothing *is* more dangerous than God's Word. These guys are right. The Bible has the power to convict the guilty and to redeem the lost. It tells of fallen humanity bound for an eternity without hope, and a redeeming Savior. The Bible releases people from condemnation and provides a plan for salvation from death.

It is His truth.

3. Mankind is eternally lost and in need of a Savior

The message of mankind's universal lostness is a tough sell. We pack arenas to hear enthusiastic speakers tell us about our great untapped potential. Motivational materials are sold to aspiring businesspeople by the truckload. Major corporations sponsor pep rallies to inspire their employees to productivity and increased sales. Even clergymen are tempted to fill their churches by preaching a gospel of "you can do it" and "faith is fun and fulfilling and good for you." Lostness and sinfulness are hard to market.

LOSTNESS AND SINFULNESS ARE HARD TO MARKET.

But just like acknowledging our hunger brings us to the dinner table, confessing our sin lifts us to a Savior. This is an essential ingredient in our preparation for the inevitability of all hell breaking loose.

Ironically, the desperation and helplessness we might *feel*, especially in the middle of a crisis, is a *fact* all the time. Without a Savior, we're lost. Getting a promotion, buying a new car, celebrating a birthday with friends, winning the big game, becoming a parent for the first time—all these are wonderful experiences. But they can sometimes conceal our sense of lostness, our certain death.

You and I are lost. We are dead in our sins. We need a Savior.

4. Jesus Christ died to redeem mankind

When Bobbie and I were newlyweds, some friends offered us their Sunfish to go sailing on Lake Michigan. If you have never seen one, a Sunfish is essentially a big surfboard with a sail. I accepted the offer without asking any questions—not even basic questions like "How does someone who has never sailed go about sailing?" I guess I didn't ask this because I was too eager to impress my bride. Not a good decision.

The day was clear, the breeze warm and just right for a small craft like ours. But the outing was a fiasco. I couldn't get the boat to do anything right. My frustration was exceeded only by my embarrassment. Making some lame excuse for why the Sunfish refused to work properly, I put the boat back, and we went home.

The next day, the owner called to see how our adventure had gone. I admitted to "some frustration." "Did you put down the centerboard?" the owner asked. Not quick enough to mask my ineptness, I replied, "What centerboard?"

Jesus Christ is history's centerboard. We affirm this every time we write the date. All the years from creation to the Nativity— Before Christ, "B.C."—are a countdown to Christ. And every year since then is *anno Domini*, "A.D."—the year of our Lord. His Incarnation divides history.

> **JESUS CHRIST IS HISTORY'S CENTERBOARD. WE AFFIRM THIS EVERY TIME WE WRITE THE DATE.**

Today, Jesus provides stability and direction in the crosswinds and perils of life. He gives us steadiness, security, power, tranquility, and strength when all hell breaks loose.

Jesus' life, death, and resurrection provide us with eternal forgiveness for our sin—foundness for our lostness—and peace with a holy God. Life without Jesus is life without direction, without companionship...without a Savior.

Life without Jesus means facing tragedy without a centerboard.

5. Faith and grace are gifts

During the early days of my career, writing promotional copy for books was one of my assignments. The experience taught me to ask the question, "So what?" If a potential customer couldn't find the answer to the "So what?" question in the first sentence or two, it was back to the drawing board.

An honest, inquiring person could read that "God is God" and "the Bible is God's Word." He could be reminded that he is "lost and in need of a Savior" and that "Jesus Christ is God." Such a person could even agree that these things are true, and still he could ask, "So what?"

But receiving the gifts of faith and grace changes everything. With faith and grace, the first four stepping stones become personal. The God of creation is *my* heavenly Father. God's Word tells *me* His story and uncovers the truth of *my* sin and salvation. *My* lostness drives me to Jesus Christ, who gave His life to be *my* Savior. I receive His grace. And like a place card on the table at a fancy dinner party, His grace has *my* name on it.

This may sound self-centered, but it's not. God's grace is meant to be poured into your heart first. Even the flight attendant tells you to put on your own oxygen mask before helping others with theirs.

But receiving this personalized gift of grace takes faith.

Jesus told the story of a woman—a widow—who had been wronged by an adversary (Luke 18:2–8). She went to an unjust judge and pleaded her own case. Day after day she ignored decorum, doing everything she could to get the judge's attention. He tried to ignore her, but Jesus says that he feared she would "wear him out" with her persistence. So he relented and heard her case, granting her the equity she deserved.

LIKE GRACE, FAITH IS A GIFT WAITING TO BE RECEIVED. AND WHEN WE RECEIVE THE GIFT OF FAITH, TRUTH BECOMES PERSONAL EXPERIENCE.

Then Jesus said, "Learn a lesson from this evil judge. Even [though the judge was unjust,] he rendered a just decision in the end, so don't you think God will surely give justice to his chosen people who plead with him day and night? Will he keep putting them off? I tell you, he will grant justice to them quickly! But when I, the Son of Man, return, how many will I find who have faith?" (Luke 18:6–8, NLT)

In telling the story, Jesus did not criticize the woman for pleading for herself and not for others. She laid claim to the judge's attention for her *own* case and believed that he would hear *her* petition. And Jesus called her persistence faith.

"I don't have that kind of faith," you might say. Of course you don't. But God *will* give it to anyone who asks. Like grace, faith is a gift waiting to be received. And when we receive the gift of faith, truth becomes personal experience.

Here's how it happens. "For if you confess with your mouth that Jesus is Lord and believe in your heart that God raised him from the dead, you will be saved. For it is by believing in your heart that you are made right with God, and it is by confessing with your mouth that you are saved." (Romans 10:9–10, NLT)

This was the verse I read to my friend, Nathan, that morning. Moments later he and I prayed together and he was saved.

6. Belief and good works
are one

For centuries an argument has raged among theologians about whether faith or good works is more important. The answer is both.

What we believe cannot—and should not—be separated from how we act. What we claim as truth ought to have a discernible effect on our behavior. Don Quixote quipped, "The proof of the pudding is in the eating," and the Apostle James put it this way: "Show me your faith without your works, and I'll show you my faith by my works." (James 2:18, NKJV)

What good is it to believe in God and the Bible and Jesus if our lives aren't in line? Our faith doesn't go dark when we're in a "heated discussion" with our spouse. This is where it should *show up*.

Our faith doesn't tiptoe away when we're out on the town with our friends. This is where it *should* show up.

We don't hit the delete key on our beliefs when we're sitting at our computer screen. This is where it *should* show up.

Our faith doesn't go dormant when all hell breaks loose. *This* is where it should show up.

"When the Holy Spirit controls our lives," Paul wrote, "*He* will produce this kind of fruit in us: love, joy, peace, patience, kindness, goodness, faithfulness, gentleness, and self-control." (Galatians 5:22–23, NLT, emphasis added)

Living out this challenging list of characteristics doesn't make us believers. But if you and I *are* Christ-followers, our lives should be marked by this fully integrated, distinct behavior. And the work that's involved is not the gutting-it-out kind, like when we're jogging that last few hundred yards. The "work" is in turning over control to God's Holy Spirit—then He does the rest.

Like ingredients poured in a mixing bowl and "beaten to a thorough consistency," our beliefs and our works become indistinguishable from each other. What we believe takes over the way we think. And our thinking is transformed because we have received God's gift of faith. For example, the evidence that we have received this gift shows up in the way we speak and act to everyone, including our spouse and children.

No hidden camera would be able to contradict who we say we are. And even in the throes of the scenarios we've talked about, our behavior when all hell is breaking loose will be consistent with who we say we are—and how we act—in the ordinary.

This is really important. Before you give up and think, "I'm not really a Christian because I keep messing up," listen to God's provision again. Because we have received God's gifts of grace and faith, we have the power to get back on track when we fail. We recognize God for who He is; we acknowledge that Jesus Christ's blood washes away our sin; we repent; we thankfully receive His grace and ask for His power to be and do what He wants.

7. The church is God's idea

So much of what we have discussed involves our individual beliefs and activities. But once the fundamentals are in place, the Christian life was never intended to be lived in isolation. Like a platoon storming a hill and attacking an enemy position in wartime, we can count on the muscle of fellow soldiers.

The church—a special community of fellow revelers during the good times and elite special forces when we're under fire—is God's idea. "[As] iron sharpens iron, so one man sharpens another." (Proverbs 27:17, NASB) Our local church is the place where we'll find this "iron."

OUR FAITH DOESN'T TIPTOE AWAY WHEN WE'RE OUT ON THE TOWN WITH OUR FRIENDS. THIS IS WHERE IT *SHOULD* SHOW UP.

BECAUSE OF THE CHURCH, WE WILL NEVER FACE TRAGEDY WITHOUT THE COMFORT OF PEOPLE GATHERED AROUND US TO SHARE IN OUR PAIN.

James adds more of God's wisdom. "Confess your sins to each other," he writes, "and pray for each other so that you may be healed. The earnest prayer of a righteous person has great power and wonderful results." (James 5:16, NLT) We find "righteous" friends at church—people with whom we can band together, learn together, and grow together. These are the comrades who will pray for us and for whom we will pray. The church is where we are taught truth and encouraged and strengthened and healed. Because of the church, we will never face tragedy without the comfort of people gathered around us to share in our pain.

In God's sovereign plan, Jesus Christ came to earth and gathered twelve men around him to share in the experience of walking together. Jesus certainly was capable of accomplishing His task all by Himself. And no doubt there were times when the disciples got in the way. But Jesus set an example for how our journey with Him should be experienced, and it wasn't alone. It was in community.

In the same way that riding out a hurricane alone is a very bad idea, living out our lives in isolation will never work. The church is God's idea.

Always Be Ready

Many years ago, in preparing to teach these "seven things," I imagined neighbors showing up at my front door and saying, "We've dabbled in Christianity, but we would like to get serious, and we'd like *you* to teach us about the basics of the Christian faith." My aim was to make the core of Christian beliefs understandable, memorable, and teachable. My inspiration was the Apostle Peter's admonition to the early church: "You must worship Christ as Lord of your life. And if you are asked about your Christian hope, always be ready to explain it." (1 Peter 13:15, NLT)

Being able to respond to the imagined neighbors at my door motivated me to try to break the basics down into bite-size pieces. But helping others to be prepared to teach the same was even more exciting.

So let's say that the neighbors are at *your* front door asking if *you* would be willing to tell them the basics of your Christian faith. Our discussion of the seven things has prepared you for this. You don't have to run for cover, desperately wishing someone else would answer the doorbell.

Another Kind of Ready

There's the sweater-in-your-suitcase ready, the storm-shutters ready, the building-on-rock ready. This is the kind of "ready" that the forecaster on the Weather Channel tells us to be when a storm is coming, the kind of "ready" that mounts a fire extinguisher in an accessible place, the kind of "ready" that teaches our youngest child how to dial 911.

As wonderful as it will be when your neighbors do ring your doorbell and you're prepared to talk about your faith, there's another kind of "ready." *Ready* is what you and I must be before all hell breaks loose. Ready with a well-equipped heart when crisis comes. The key is to anticipate the crisis, not waiting till it's too late to have these things nailed down. We need a plan before the emergency is upon us.

Following the attacks of September 11, 2001, members of Congress gathered on the Capitol steps. All hell had certainly broken loose that day. The most powerful legislative body on the face of the earth would eventually lay out a plan for a military response, but before that happened, they lifted their voices in song. "God bless America," they sang, "Land that I love. Stand beside her and guide her through the night with the light from above."

To an outsider, that might have seemed like a pathetically impotent gesture. But we know that in the moment it was the most important thing they could have done. Preparing ourselves for hell's breaking loose by nailing down the basic truths is not an exercise in futility. It's the most important thing we can do.

A New Kind of Dangerous

The most sobering and perilous dimensions of terrorist fear around the world are encapsulated in two words: *suicide bomber*. Decades before we learned of this horrible wartime strategy, James A. Baldwin summarized the threat this way: "The most dangerous creation of any society is the man who has nothing to lose."[2]

Goliath the Philistine knew something about this sort of jeopardy. One morning in the valley of Elah, this giant warrior stood in shameless defiance of the army of the living God, to which he had issued a challenge: "Choose a man for yourselves, and let him come down to me. If he is able to fight with me and kill me, then we will be your servants; but if I prevail against him and kill him, then you shall be our servants and serve us." (1 Samuel 17:8–9) After forty days of Goliath's taunts, the boy David took up his challenge and went out to meet him armed with two weapons: a simple slingshot and nothing to lose.

"You come to me with a sword, a spear, and a javelin," David shouted to Goliath, "but I come to you in the name of the LORD of hosts, the God of the armies of Israel, whom you have taunted." (1 Samuel 17:45, NASB)

David knew what you and I know.

Preparing ourselves for the hell that will come crashing down on us is about one thing only—holding on to what is true. What we know about God and His word, what we believe about our lostness, our faith in the redemptive power of Jesus to save us, and the collective power of His people gathered together.

"THE MOST DANGEROUS CREATION OF ANY SOCIETY IS THE MAN WHO HAS NOTHING TO LOSE."

There is nothing else we need. This is truth worth dying for.

In the face of death, Paul asserted, "I myself no longer live, but Christ lives in me." (Galatians 2:20) "Go ahead and *let* hell break loose," Paul defiantly declared. "You can't kill me. I'm already dead!" When these truths are ours, we have everything to gain and nothing to lose, even during great crisis or unthinkable pressure.

As a boy, lying on the floor behind an overstuffed chair and reading *Foxe's Book of Martyrs*, I was filled with awe for the people who courageously faced their own deaths rather than succumb to the demands of their captors. These martyrs joined many heroes who had gone before and became a cloud of witnesses to cheer me on.

Fortified only with what they knew to be true and the faith to face hell itself, these people changed the course of history.

Now Nathan and you and I can join them.

ACKNOWLEDGMENTS

E ven though I've made a living in other pursuits, building construction has almost been a way of life since I was eighteen years old and got my first taste of the business. Adventures of tackling projects have been recorded in scrapbooks that are...hmmmm, let's see. After several moves in the past few years, I'm not exactly sure where the scrapbooks are. They must be somewhere. Anyway, it's true. Lots of projects.

Almost all of the construction things I've accomplished have been connected to our family. Serious building was first launched with my daughters, Missy and Julie, when they were young. And then, after they were married, with their husbands, Jon and Christopher.

During the summer of 2016, as I was going through the editorial rigors of finishing, submitting, editing, rewriting and editing this manuscript again, I took on two building projects. The first was the expansion of the deck on the back of our house. The deck used to be 500 square feet. Now it's a thousand and has already played host to many celebrations.

The second was a much smaller adventure, laying and mortaring 60 seventy-pound cut flagstones onto the concrete porch on the front of the house.

Going back to soliciting my kids and their husbands as apprentices...what I still know about building projects is that, even though I may be the guy with the idea and may even be the one with the most experience or daring, I cannot—would not—tackle them by myself.

I always find someone...or two...to come along side and help. This makes the job go more efficiently and smoothly and safely and, actually, it makes the experience a lot more memorable. Even enjoyable.

From the time the first paragraph is drafted for the book proposal that is submitted to publishing houses, all the way to hitting the "send" key on the final, final edit, every author brings people along side. Sometims lots of them. This truly is my story as well.

As I mentioned in this book, the idea for this manuscript came from a dinner conversation I had early in 2015 with my friend, Nancy Leigh DeMoss. Over grilled salmon, I said, "For years, your ministry has inspired the idea of biblical womanhood. You have lovingly challenged hundreds of thousands of wives to 'let your husbands lead.' But what about these men? Who is going to tell them? Who is going to motivate them to accept this amazing challenge?" In that moment, this book was born.

I am thankful to Nancy—now my precious wife, confidant, and personal manuscript editor—not only from the moment this idea was conceived but all the way to the end when, as I mentioned above, I hit the "send" key on the document for the final time.

I'm also grateful for Missy and Julie, for their love and support all these years, now deep into our fifth decade together. Of course, their mother and my wife for almost 45 years, Bobbie, first shaped in my mind many of the concepts you'll find in this book...and these came from her thorough and relentless study of God's Word. Thank you to Bobbie.

Missy and Julie's husbands, Jon Schrader and Christopher Tassy, are wonderful husbands and loyal friends to me. And I cannot forget my amazing grandchildren: Abby Schrader, Luke Schrader, Isaac Schrader, Harper Tassy, and Ella Tassy. I thank them.

As the manuscript was taking its final form, several friends dove in to help. Tim Challies, Mark Hayes, Dale Alexander and Dale Murphy were most helpful.

My publisher, Regnery Faith, is crowded with consummate professionals: Marji Ross, Tom Spence (my editor), Gary Terashita (and Bob DeMoss, Gary's predecessor), Alyssa Cordova, Lauren MacDonald, Emily Beasley, and John Caruso.

I hail from a large family...almost 100 strong at this moment. This large family is so large because my parents—mostly my mother, Grace—had six kids. These siblings and their mates are still among our closest friends and I'm so thankful for them: Stan and Ruth Guillaume, Sam and Mary Gayle Wolgemuth, Ken and Sharon Wolgemuth, Dan and Mary Wolgemuth and Debbie Birkey. These people are so special...the older we get, the closer we become.

When Nancy and I married in November 2015, I became part of her family...her mother—whom I gratefully call "Mother" since my own stepped into heaven in 2010—her sisters, Charlotte, Deborah (and her husband Rene), and Elisabeth and her brothers Mark (and his wife April) and Paul.

And I was adopted into a bonus clan...Nancy's ministry family. These people have been incredibly kind in welcoming me to Michigan and I have been deeply blessed by these new friendships, among them: Stacey Battenburg, Sandy Bixel, Jim and Linda Bever, Nathan and Katie Bollinger, Hugh and Renae Duncan, Del and Debra Fehsenfeld and their sweet children, Dennis and Carrie Gaul, Debbie Hancock, Dan and Melissa Jarvis, Martin and Helen Jones, Phil and Christy Krause, Hannah Kurtz, Dawn Leuschen, Tom and Kim Mathis, Nate and Robyn McLaurin, Mike and Chris Neises, Aaron and Victoria Paulus, Brent and Maggie Paulus, Byron and Sue Paulus (and their dozen precious grandchildren), Nate and Jess Paulus, Leanna Shepard, Mindy Sherwood, Tom and Carla Shier, Tom and Roz Sullivan, Angela Temples, Monica Vaught, Ed and Gayle Villalba, Graham Ward, and Bill and Tammy Zebell.

Nancy has seven close women friends who all call themselves, "The Sisterhood." From the early days of my courtship with Nancy, these women have been very special. Because they have also become friends and, may I say, cheerleaders, for Nancy's husband, I thankfully adding them to this list of folks to whom I express my deepest thanks.

For well over a decade, my pastor, Dr. David Swanson, was my self-appointed "wingman." The Scripture refers to men like this as "a friend that sticks closer than a brother." This perfectly describes David. I'm very thankful for him.

More often than not, an author will thank his or her agent in the Acknowledgments. This time, my agents are also my colleagues with Wolgemuth & Associates, and their significant help with this project…and my day to day life and work…could never be exaggerated: Andrew Wolgemuth, Erik Wolgemuth, Austin Wilson and Susan Kreider. Thank you all.

Thank you to Michael Hyatt, my soul brother and former business partner for almost sixteen years. The only person I asked for an endorsement, Mike was gracious enough to lend his good name and kind words to the cover of this book.

I am grateful to Jesus Christ, the Good Shepherd. His guidance and care has been this wayward lamb's salvation. Literally. And I will be eternally grateful for His love. Literally.

Finally, I'm grateful to you, the reader of this book. The fact that you'd spend a few hours reading what I've pounded out here is quite overwhelming to me. And I sincerely trust that these hours will provide a sweet ROI in your life, your marriage and your home.

Robert Wolgemuth

NOTES

ONE: NO TURNING BACK

I'm aware that, as a man, Cortés was no paragon of virtue. Far from it. He may have been courageous as an explorer, but history reports that he was not a faithful husband and his theology was a disaster...conducting this adventure to win God's favor. Some have charged Cortés with blatant and inexcusable racism in his conquests. These things are clearly without excuse, but if you'll forgive me, I'd still like to use this story to make a point.

1. Aesop, *Fables*, retold by Joseph Jacobs, Vol. XVII, Part 1, The Harvard Classics (New York: P. F. Collier & Son, 1909–14); Bartleby.com, 2001.www.bartleby.com/17/1/.

2. http://www.biblebb.com/files/spurgeon/0762.htm

TWO: SHEEP

1. Some of this information was borrowed from Dr. David P. Murray, Old Testament and Practical Theology professor at Puritan Reformed Theological Seminary. He is a very bright man and was born in Scotland where the thistle is their national symbol and there are more sheep than people...almost seven million vs. just over five million. The country also has over seven hundred islands, which is fortunate for sheep attempting to wander away from home. Sheep can swim. http://www.sermonaudio.com/sermoninfo.asp?SID=212111156369

2. http://goo.gl/O9gk4t

3. Soon after the announcement about my firm representing NLD again, a prominent publisher in our industry tweeted, "Some guys will do anything to re-sign an author client!"

FIVE: A SHEPHERD KNOWS HIS SHEEP

1. Barbara Brown Taylor, *The Preaching Life* (Lanham, Md.: Rowman & Littlefield, 1993), pp. 146–147.

2. George Will, "Nature and the Male Sex," *Newsweek*, June 17, 1991.

SIX: A SHEPHERD SPEAKS TO HIS SHEEP

1. Genesis 45:3.

2. Robert Wolgemuth, *She Calls Me Daddy: 7 Things You Need to Know about Building a Complete Daughter*, paperback reprint edition (Colorado Springs: Focus on the Family, 2014), 59.

3. Albert Mehrabian, *Nonverbal Communication*, (New Brunswick, N.J.: Aldine Transaction, 1972), 182.

SEVEN: A SHEPHERD SATISFIES HIS SHEEP

1. DreamBuilders (www.dreambuildersnetwork.com) was founded in 2004 by my friend Kennan Burch. Through this "undercover network of friends," God has faithfully given us the joy of dreaming big dreams and telling each other about them.
2. "So when the woman saw that the tree was good for food, and that it was a delight to the eyes, and that the tree was to be desired to make one wise, she took of its fruit and ate, and she also gave some to *her husband who was with her,* and he ate." (Genesis 3:6, emphasis added)

TEN: A SHEPHERD COMFORTS HIS SHEEP

1. Phillip Keller, *A Shepherd Looks at Psalm 23* (Grand Rapids, Mich.: Zondervan, 1970).

ELEVEN: A SHEPHERD FEEDS HIS SHEEP

1. Janis Frawley-Holler, "The Sacred Table," *Family Circle,* 8 October 2002, p. 210.
2. https://www.goodreads.com/author/quotes/2876959.Charles_Haddon_Spurgeon
3. Out of respect and sheer awe, some Jews do not write out the sacred name of "God," omitting the vowel. Although Christians have no qualms about spelling out God's whole name, the Jewish practice is a powerful example of reverence. See Isaiah 6:1–7.

TWELVE: A SHEPHERD ENCOURAGES HIS SHEEP

1. Albert Willemetz, Charles Lucien, Maurice Jacques-Yvain Copyright © 1965, EMI Music Publishing, Sony/ATV Music Publishing LLC, Universal Music Publishing Group. Bobbie changed the fourth line when she sang it to me.

2. Joshua Wolf Shenk, "The Power of Two," *The Atlantic*, July–August 2014, http://www.theatlantic.com/magazine/archive/2014/07/the-power-of-two/372289/; see also, idem, *Powers of Two: Finding the Essence of Innovation in Creative Pairs* (New York: Houghton Mifflin Harcourt, 2014).

THIRTEEN: A SHEPHERD MEETS THE NEEDS OF HIS SHEEP

1. These concepts are identified and expanded on in Robert Wolgemuth and Mark DeVries, *The Most Important Year in a Man's Life* (Nashville: Thomas Nelson Publishers, 2003).

FOURTEEN: A SHEPHERD PASTORS HIS SHEEP

1. http://www.ccel.org/ccel/wesley/journal.vi.ii.xvi.html
2. Most trustworthy biblical scholars agree that, in the New Testament, "elder," "pastor," and "shepherd" are interchangeable terms. So in this text, Peter is talking to you and me.
3. Thanks to Dr. John MacArthur for some of these helpful thoughts.

FIFTEEN: LOVE FOR A LIFETIME: FINISHING WELL

1. Daniel Iverson, 1926 copyright © 1982, Hope Publishing Company, Carol Stream, IL. Dr. Iverson's son, William, performed the wedding ceremony for Nancy's parents, Art and Nancy DeMoss, in 1957.

APPENDIX: HOW TO EMBRACE THE GOOD SHEPHERD AS YOUR GOOD SHEPHERD

1. C. S. Lewis, *Mere Christianity* (New York: Macmillan, 1952), pp. 164–165.
2. James A. Baldwin, *Collected Essays* (New York: Library of America, 1998), p. 330.